Inspired Beauty

How the Aesthetics of White Features Influenced the World

SILAS C. WOLFE

ISBN 979-8-89112-744-9 (Paperback)
ISBN 979-8-89112-745-6 (Digital)

First Edition

Covenant Books
11661 Hwy 707
Murrells Inlet, SC 29576
www.covenantbooks.com

To the Father, the Son, and the Holy Spirit

CONTENTS

PREFACE

This book is not intended to discriminate against any nationality, race, color, or creed. The inspiration for writing this book was the revelation God has given me—to search for the truth of the origins of the Aryan race and why other cultures are obsessed with looking thin or fair skinned.

At a very young age and up until adulthood, I've always been fascinated with the unexplained mysterious of this world, searching for the truth of how things originated and why things are the way they are today. Looking back at my past, as a little child, I was always into watching sci-fi movies, like *Star Wars*, *Star Trek*, *The X-Files*, and *X-Men*. These movies kept me interested, and I would ask myself, "Do ghosts, demons, angels, and extraterrestrial life really exist beyond this world, and if they do, do they still live among us? Why?"

To my knowledge, in 2012, God revealed to me secrets about the Aryan race. They were a supernatural race made perfect in beauty and intelligence by God (Ezekiel 28:14), and they were destined to be God's heavenly messengers in heaven. The Aryan gods' mission here on earth was to be the watchers of mankind on the earth until one day, pride over took their leader, Samyaza, causing two-thirds of the angels to be cast out of heaven. Just imagine, these higher beings, the most beautiful and of higher intelligence, came from the heavens and were able to teach mankind the art of farming, arts, crafts, science, astrology, and language, then manipulated the human races with their supernatural powers, ruling over mankind as the most high in the form of gods, goddess, leaders, and kings on the earth today. From the pre-Adamic ages on earth, Adam's bloodline was the original dark-skinned races on earth who were made in the image of God to inhabit the earth. That was until the angels rebelled against God, lusting after the sons of man on planet Earth (Genesis 6:2–4), causing the races of mankind on earth to appear lighter than the others.

In addition to biblical evidence, the book of Numbers 12:1–2 and Kings 5:27 explain that the true original Israelites, who were God's chosen people, were of dark completion because every time one of the biblical characters disobeyed God, God cursed them with white leprosy, causing their skin to turn snow white. Even though dark skin was considered in the 1880s by leaders of the scientific community as a curse, white skin in the biblical times of the Old Testament (Enoch 106:14, Numbers 12:1) was seen as curse or peculiar.

From the heavens, the angels acted as godlike beings on the earth, where they appeared to the human races as sun gods, having the appearance of the sun and the sky. Descriptively, the sky gods appeared to the human races as illuminated beings similar to the bright sun (Isaiah 14:12–17), having blond hair that was golden like the sun, blue eyes as beautiful as the blue sky, and pale-white skin that similar to white clouds. During the Sumerian ages, sun worship became a common practice in Peru, Mexico, Egypt, and China, where the sun acted as a source of divinity or a guide for many different purposes; it helped grow food, functioned as a cornerstone in creating calendars, enabled the telling of time, and acted as a compass for navigation. When the Aryan gods visited the different tribes on earth, they were worshipped for their godlike or sunlike appearance, and many statues were made to idolize or worship these Aryan gods. Over time, mankind was deceived into believing these sun gods were like the Most High, Yahweh, and many of our history books (even biblical books) in Rome and England were rewritten or painted over to make us believe the true Messiah was White. On the contrary, he was Black. Furthermore, Greek and Roman cultures idolized the Olympian gods, the Greeks and Romans imitating them in many forms of poetry, philosophy, architecture, statues, and paintings, which became the catalyst of the development of Western culture. Throughout time, European imperialism has often diminished and overshadowed the beauty and existence of other cultures, brainwashing them into believing that the aesthetics, values, and cultures associated with Whiteness are the pinnacle of appeal in our society today.

INSPIRED BEAUTY CHART

Sky gods

Greek culture

Western philosophy

Architecture

Statues

Paintings

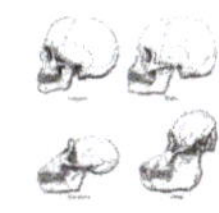
Scientific racism

Master race

Standard of beauty

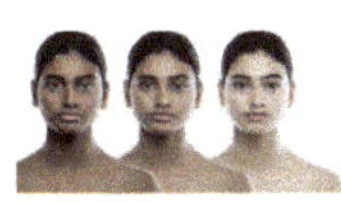
Effects of Westernization

Sky gods. The sky gods were created perfect in beauty and intelligence by God, then cast out of heaven because of their rebellion against Yahweh (Ezekiel 28:12–17).

Greek culture. The Greeks revered the Olympian gods for their divine powers, imitating them in many forms of art, from architecture to statues to paintings to dramas to philosophy.

Western philosophy. Pythagoras discovered the golden ratio, inspiring many architects, sculptors, and painters, to design their artwork in accordance to proportional perfection. Botticelli, da Vinci, Raphael, and Michelangelo helped shape humanism through their artwork and defined Western philosophy.

Architecture. The temples in Ancient Greece represented the Aryan form and were well proportioned in accordance to the golden ratio.

Statues. Statues from the classical period to the neoclassical period represented the Aryan gods in their secular form—athletic and beautiful.

Paintings. Paintings from the classical period to the neoclassical period represented images of the Aryan gods in human form as deities ruling over mankind.

Scientific racism. Darwin helped shaped the racial superiority in the nineteenth century; his theories suggested that the White race was superior to all other races in mind, body, and intelligence.

Master race. Darwin's ideology on race influenced Hitler, who stated that the Aryan race was superior to all other races, and that the blond-hair, blue-eyed appeal became the standard of beauty in Europe.

Standards of beauty. In the 1930s, Betty Grable and Marlene Dietrich came from the German film industry and into Hollywood, influencing the "blonde-haired sex symbol" archetype worldwide.

Effects of Westernization. Eastern and Western cultures are have been heavily influenced to conform to the Eurocentric standard of beauty.

HISTORY OF INSPIRED BEAUTY

<<TBD>>	<<TBD>>
3000 BC	The Anunnaki came from the heavens to earth and were worshipped by mankind as sun gods.
3000–2500 BC	The sky gods landed in the land of Canaan (Mount Hermon) and mated with human women, resulting in Aryan giants (Nephilim). The sky gods were also responsible for the engineering of the Aryan race of humans.
2500–2000 BC	Majority of the Aryan races (Celtic races) migrated from the Middle East and settled in the northern parts of Europe.
2000–1600 BC	Minoan culture was evidently the first European culture to inspire Western art.
1981 BC–1971 BC	Helen was abducted, and the Trojan War began and ended.
1600–1200 BC	The Minoan culture vanished; and the early Minoans migrated to Mycenae, where the Greeks told many myths about the Olympian gods, imitated the gods in many different forms of art, and brought forth Western philosophy.
854 BC	Italy was founded.
800 BC	Homer was the first Greek poet who recounted stories of the beautiful ancient gods that ruled in Mycenaean Greece.
776 BC	The Olympics was created to pay homage to the gods.
700 BC	The Ionic order was the first architectural order to appear in Ancient Greece.
620 BC	Thales was the first Greek mathematician and philosopher in Greece who helped inspire Pythagoras's ideas on the golden ratio.

570 BC	Pythagoras inspired many philosophers, sculptors, painters, and architects into believing that all things are numbers, based on the mathematical beauty of the golden ratio.
509 BC	The Roman Empire was founded.
500 BC–400 BC	The classical period began and ended.
336 BC	Alexander the Great was the first Aryan ruler who conquered many vast empires, from Persia to Asia Minor, spreading European philosophies to other countries.
30 BC	Vitruvius wrote the book *De architectura*.
29 BC	Virgil, a Roman poet, translated the Olympian gods' names into Latin.
27 BC	Augustus Caesar, founded the Roman Empire.
AD 1	Jesus Christ was born.
AD 8	Ovid published his book titled *Metamorphoses*.
AD 395	Christianity became the official religion of the Roman Empire.
1066 BC– AD 1480	The medieval period started and ended.
AD 1020	Fibonacci was a mathematician who created the Fibonacci principle.
AD 1400–1600	The Renaissance period began and ended.
AD 1440	The *Birth of Venus* was painted by Botticelli.
AD 1500	Many Florentine painters—like da Vinci, Raphael, and Michelangelo—created their philosophy on physical beauty.
AD 1400–1960	The Westernization period started and ended.
AD 1750–1860	The neoclassical period began and ended.
AD 1859	Darwin's book *On the Origin of Species* helped shaped racial superiority, European imperialism, and Nazi ideology.
AD 1874–1914	European imperialism began and ended.
AD 1933–1946	The Nazis spread the blond-hair, blue-eyed aesthetic appeal through many Hollywood films.
AD 1930	Television helped depict the iconic beauty of White American actors and actresses.
Twenty-first century	The average model is tall, thin, or fair skinned. The effects of Westernization have brainwashed other cultures into changing their looks into appearing more Western.

CHAPTER 1

Defining Beauty

What is beauty?

Beauty is an object that creates a visual or sensual experience of pleasure within a person. Famous philosophers Socrates and Plato quoted their own ideas on beauty, stating that "beauty has no certain restrictions. It can come in all shapes, forms, or sizes, and whatever a person view is beautiful, then it is beautiful." Taking a look at our world every day, we see beauty all around us—from the flowers, plants, and trees in our backyards to the scenic Rocky Mountains in the Midwest to the tallest mountain, Mount Everest, in Asia to the aging rocks of the Grand Canyon to the magnificent water of Niagara Falls to the array of species in the Amazon Rainforest to the exotic beaches in the Bermuda. Even the constellations of the stars at night are forms of aesthetics. Other forms of aesthetics can be found in the language or sounds of music from living things. The different languages in the world can be translated into many different forms—from English to Spanish to French to Portuguese to Italian to Chinese to Japanese to Korean to Hindi to Nigerian to Jamaican to Arabian to Latin—which brings a uniquely different form of dialect to each language. The different musical instruments people use to make sound produce music that is pleasing to the mind, body, and soul. Moreover, professional vocalist like Celine Dion and Whitney Houston have aesthetic appeals in their vocals, and the chirping of birds in the wild helps birds communicate to defend their territories, among other things. These sounds are like musical singing to the human ears. In our homes, everyday materials we use can appear beautiful to us—from the suits and dresses we wear, which can be made out of a certain design, to the jewelry we put on to the cars we drive to the gadgets we use to communicate, such as the smartphone, computer, and HD TV (they are ever changing into sleeker and slimmer designs).

Beauty in other cultures

In cultures around the world, beauty can come in many different forms. In Northern Thailand, young women at an early age wear brass coils around their neck to deform the clavicle and elongate their necks. An elongated neck is considered beautiful. In India, a bright red dot, called the bindi, is applied to the middle of the forehead of men, women, and children. According to the ancient Hindu religion, the bindi signifies the third eye (chakra), representing an entry into a heightened state of consciousness and deeper connection with the spiritual realm. Today, in some parts of India, a majority of women wear the bindi to signify marriage, prosperity, or status and even for decorative purposes—to enhance the beauty of a woman. In China, foot-binding was a widespread tradition in which all women, regardless of social class, wrapped their feet in bandages and confined them to small shoes. Over time, their feet became slimmer. To the Chinese at that time, this symbolized a woman's moral virtue, beauty, and allure to men. In Kenya, the Maasai tribe wear animal skins on their bodies and possess elongated earlobes. The elongated earlobes adorned with elephant tusks are a symbol of beauty in the Maasai tribe. In New Zealand, the Maori tribe wear tattoos called mokos, and the tradition of mokos goes way back, even before the Europeans arrived in New Zealand. The tattoos for men and women are symbols of beauty. In France, women age naturally until old age rather than wear a lot of cosmetics (makeup). Women in France believe aging naturally brings out your true beauty. In American mainstream media, the all-American look has often been portrayed as the epitome of beauty: tall, thin, fair skinned, with chiseled features, high cheekbones, and light-colored eyes and hair. This portrayal has significantly influenced global perceptions of beauty standards.

The aesthetics of light

When God formed the earth, he separated daytime from nighttime, allowing daytime to be light and night to be dark. Moreover, look at the effect light can have on living things. Light acts as a simulator, generating energy in the cells of living organisms—from human brains and skin to plants and microorganisms. For example, when light is absorbed into human skin, we get vitamin D, which helps keep our bones strong. Clinically, light therapy through the pupil to the optic nerve has shown promise in helping patients with Alzheimer's on Epilepsy to better control their brain functions, enhancing memory and learning clarity.

Seasonal affective disorder is an illness that is more prevalent in the winter months, from November up until April, which is when a person receives less sunlight. They become sad due to the longer and darker nights of winter because the amount of melatonin, produced by the pineal gland (in the brain), increases, which causes sadness and depression. Serotonin is the opposite to melatonin; serotonin is a neurotransmitter in the brain that affects the way we feel in a positive way. When a person is around more sunlight, their serotonin levels increases in their brains, causing them to feel happier, cheerful, and confident. Interestingly enough, we know that everybody is attracted to beautiful weather, like a sunny day in the spring; and when there's more sunshine, people get less sleep and are more energized because the sun changes our mood, causing us to be more active. (We move around and get more exercise in the summer compared to winter.)

Other than the sunlight, bright city lights at night are proven to increase serotonin in our brains. For instance, when going down the busy Las Vegas Strip at night, you see the energy in the atmosphere: lots of people roaming the streets, interacting with other people, gambling at casinos, staying at a hotel, hanging out with their friends, or taking a stroll along the Strip. The bright lights at night are designed to attract potential customers for the casinos and resorts to stay in business. The businesses use an array of advertisements and emblems, along with bright lights, that immediately draw attention to the potential gambler or hotel guest. If there were no bright lights at night along the Las Vegas Strip, then everything would be lifeless; the bright lights bring life to the Las Vegas Strip, helping the casino business boom. Major cities across the world—like New York, San Francisco, Seattle, Shanghai, Tokyo, Dubai, London, and Sydney—all have the most stunning skyscrapers in the world. When you go sightseeing at night and see these tall buildings, you'll become mesmerized by the height and elegant architectural design as well as the beautiful bright lights that shine off these tall structures.

Overall, light therapy has provided a solution to people with seasonal affective disorder. For example, a lighted lamp helps people cope with their depression and increases the serotonin levels in their brain. The effects of bright light are amazing, and so is how sunshine can affect a person's mood or behavior.

Biblical verses on physical beauty

First Samuel 16:7 says the world judges you based on your outward beauty, but God judges your heart.

In 1 Samuel 3:6, God says it's more important to keep a righteous, humble heart than be concerned with your outward beauty.

Isaiah 40:7 says that a man's beauty will fade away, like how a flower, from spring to fall, withers, but God's Word stands forever.

Proverbs 6:25 says that a man shouldn't lust after a women's beauty in his heart.

Proverbs 31:30 says that charm and beauty are not important in God's view; a woman who fears the Lord is more important.

CHAPTER 2

Origins of the Aryan Race

Sky gods

Illustration 1

From the spirit world came the fallen angels, who came from the heavens and visited the earth. As the angels descended upon the earth, they appeared to the original tribe of human races as sun gods, having the appearance of the sun and the sky—blond or reddish hair like the sun, blue eyes as beautiful as the blue sky, and pale-white skin similar to the white clouds. The book of Enoch 106:1–17, which describes Noah's birth, talks about Noah's father, Lamech, describing the appearance of Noah's albinism being similar to that of the angels' appearance; he had a skin tone that was white and ruddy, eyes that were brightly colored, and hair that was very fair. These features are similar to those of Nordic White people. The Zulus, Native Americans, Aztecs, Incas, and Peruvians, the original humans on earth, called these sky gods many different names—from Quetzalcoatl to Kukulkan to Viracocha to Gucumatz. They were sky-godlike beings with good looks and superintelligence. (They were able to teach mankind advanced knowledge in magic, sorcery, farming, science, arts, crafts, language, and warfare and were responsible for the creation of the human race, according to ancient Sumerian text.) Many of the different tribes on earth revered these sky-like beings for their bestowal of knowledge to mankind, and many statues (see image 1) were made to idolize and worship these gods. Over time, these fallen angels (Genesis 6:2–4) procreated with the sons of men on earth, resulting in an offspring known as the Nephilim, often described as giants. These giants became mighty rulers on earth, ruling over mankind through the ages.

Aryan giants

There were angels from the spirit world that mated with women on earth, resulting in an offspring described as giants (Genesis 6:4). Egyptian, Indian, Buddhist, and Greek mythology prove this to be real; there were mighty men reaching heights of seven to thirty-six feet who helped build great monuments located in the Mediterranean—from the Great Pyramids in Egypt to the Tower of Babel in Israel to the walls of Troy in Greece to the Stonehenge in England. Five thousand years later, archeologist found evidence of giants existing far from the Mediterranean, where the ancient gods once descended upon. Significant findings include large pyramids, like those in the Tarim Basin in China and in Peru. One prime example is a mummy called the Sleeping Beauty of Loulan, found along the Desert of Xinjiang, China. She is depicted as a tall Caucasian women with keen features and long red hair (image 1). Alongside the Sleeping Beauty of Loulan is the Cherchen man, who stood about six feet tall and also had red hair. In Lima, Peru, there is evidence of mummies existing in tombs, reaching six to seven feet in height, with blond hair (image 3).

Image 1
The Sleeping Beauty of Loulan

Illustration 1
Cherchen Man

Image 2
The blonde-haired mummies in Lima, Peru

Aryan humans

A brief history. The first appearance of white skin wasn't until three hundred thousand years ago in Europe and Southwest and Central Asia. The Neanderthals went extinct thirty thousand years later because of the intermixing with the *Homo sapiens*, creating a new species called the Cro-Magnon man. The Neanderthal very much resembles the White Nordic humans that exist in Europe today; they had White features ranging from a rosy-red complexion to straight hair (blond or red) to blue or green eyes. The only difference is the that certain physical features of the Aryan race (like the head, the nose, and the lips) are much keener than the physical features of the Neanderthals. Today, if you are of European or Asian descent, then around 2 to 9 percent of your genomes originated from the Neanderthals.

Around five thousand to six thousand years ago, the second wave of Whites appeared in the land of Canaan, now called the Middle East. They are called the Aryan race. They are part Anunnaki and part human. The Tuatha Dé Danann are from the tribe of Dan, located in the northern parts of Israel, in the land of Canaan or Magog, and are said to be fourth wave of red-haired giants to inhabit Ireland (Illustration 1). Around 2500 BC, the tribe of Dan was exiled out of the land of Canaan during the great flood and migrated on ships to Ireland and Scotland. Sometime later, the Gaels and Milesians were the last race of Celtics to intermingle with the Tuatha Dé Danann, resulting in the creation of the Irish races.

In the Bible, the Gomer people are the German and British races, described as tall in stature, with blond hair and blue eyes. In reference to Hosea 1:10, the Gomer people were exiled from the land of Israel for idolatry and the practice of false worship (Norse religion) and then later appeared in the land of Magog, now known as Syria. The Gomer people were a warrior tribe that conquered many territories around the Assyrian and Persian Empires, then migrated westward from Magog to England, France, Great Britain, Germany, Norway, Sweden, and Iceland.

Celtic mythology. Over the centuries, many early inhabitants of Ireland fought against other tribal Celtic races to gain control over Ireland. The Firbolgs were the third tribe of the Celtic race to arrive in Ireland. They were a warrior tribe of people with bountiful crops and land until the Tuatha Dé Danann defeated the Firbolgs, pushing them out of Ireland.

The Tuatha Dé Danann are a supernatural race renowned for their mastery in druidry, magic, prophecy, sorcery, and weaponry, and they are descendants from the sky goddess Danu. The great kings, princes, princess, and warriors of Tara are Nuada, Bres, Lugh, Midir, Etain, Eochai, and Airem. They were beautiful youthful leaders that kept their youth until old age because of their majestic powers of the Danu people. Long after, the Tuatha Dé Danann were defeated by the Milesians, and many of the Danann tribe retreated to underground, in the underworld, called Sidhe. The Danann people kept their contact with the Milesian people on land in spirit form as well as the natural form. Many legends of the Danu people were talked about in story form—from tales of beautiful, youthful women appearing to men in spirit forms (such as the story of the island of women) to the story of a wealthy farmer called Crunnchu.

The most popular legend ever told was the great warrior Cú Chulainn. Cú Chulainn was known for his enormous strength; he was able to take on fifty men at once and defeated many great warriors in the land of Ireland. Cú Chulainn mastered weaponry and had a great fighting ability, which made him one of the best, equivalent to the Roman legend Hercules. In addition to his great fighting ability, Cú Chulainn was a beautiful warrior known to be very tall, with red hair and blue eyes.

According to Norse mythology, the Æsirs were a beautiful race of gods similar to the Nordic people, existing a long time ago (around the dark ages, AD 1000–1240) in Iceland. After the Æsirs were formed from ice, they slayed the frost giant Ymir. The Æsirs knew they were destined to live for only a short amount of time, so they played, feasted, and fought among themselves in preparation for the final battle in Vigrid, against the evil frost giants. Odin was the chief god who possessed many powers of magic, prophecy, poetry, and warfare. Odin created a warrior class of humans to rule with him in Asgard. Frigg was a goddess equivalent to the Roman goddess Venus. Freya's beauty was stunning to many men; they wanted to either sleep with her or marry her. Thor was the oldest son of Odin. He was known to be a powerful warrior and possessed a hammer, along with a belt and gloves he wore to gain the strength that could wreak havoc on the frost giants.

CHAPTER 3

Greek Culture

History of Greek and Roman culture

The Minoan culture became the first European civilization to exist during the Bronze Age. It helped shape Greek culture in government, religion, philosophy, science, entertainment, and art. As the early Minoans migrated from the Minoan Island to the Mycenaean island, the Greeks continued to trade with the Egyptians and imitated much of their culture. If you take a look back to Ancient Egypt, the Egyptian culture was the first civilization to exist on Earth, around 5000 BC. Mankind started to migrate outward from areas of the Middle East onto other continents, taking ideas from the Egyptian culture and spreading them to form their own cultures. The similarities between the Egyptian and Greek cultures are that the people loved their gods for their divine powers and began idolizing them in many artistic forms—from pottery and statues to paintings.

Some of the Egyptian statues, made out of stone, are similar to the Cycladic statues made in Amorgos. The Mycenaean culture represented many of the statue figures, like Athena, Hera, Apollo, and Diana, which were similar to the original kouros statues in Egypt that represented youthful beauty. The material used to make these sculptures was white marble, intended to show the aesthetic appeal of the gods and used in temples for idol worshipping or occult sacrificing. Other imitations of Egyptian culture include Greek painting. The "Ladies in Blue" is very similar to the side-view figures of the painting *Tomb of Nebamum*; the hand pottery made by the Egyptians is similar to the one-dimensional figures on Greek pottery. The architectural orders in Greece are similar to the Egyptian columns.

After the Roman Empire was founded in 509 BC, many great innovators such as Thales, Pythagoras, Socrates, Plato, Aristotle, and Alexander the Great became the forefathers of Western philosophy. For example, the Pythagorean theorem inspired many artists to design everything in perfect proportions, as seen in the Parthenon and the Doryphoros of Polykleitos, which were created in relation to the golden ratio. Then in 323 BC, Alexander the Great became the first Westerner to spread Greek philosophies into other cultures, influencing them to adopt classical art. After the classical period came to a short end around 400 BC, it was reinvented in AD 1400 during the Renaissance, when philosophers and painters in Florence, Italy, embarked on a new age of enlightenment. During the Renaissance period, the ideas of the wealthy class overruled the doctrines of the Roman Catholic Church. Many philosophers and painters—like da Vinci, Botticelli, Michelangelo, and Raphael—imitated their subjects in their secular form of beauty, according to the golden ratio, which transpired into the philosophical theme of the Renaissance, "that outward beauty defines a person's inner character and moral goodness." Later, this philosophical theme on beauty was philosophized throughout the rest of the world, from the fourteenth century up until the mid-nineteenth century, when Westernization ended.

Egyptian Art versus Greek Art	
Egyptian statue	Cycladic statue
Egyptian statue	Kouros statues
One-dimensional figures	One-dimensional figures
Egyptian Women Dancing	Minoan queen's fresco
Egyptian columns	Greek architectural orders

Greek and Roman mythology

A brief history. According to Greek mythology, Eros was the primal god of love, who brought about the formation of the earth, living things, and the union between Gaia and Uranus. Gaia, personified as Mother Earth, then supernaturally gave birth to Uranus, the sky god and her husband. Mating with him, she gave rise to the Titans: Oceanus, Hyperion, Coeus, Crius, Iapetus, Theia, Rhea, Themis, Mnemosyne, Phoebe, Tethys, Cronus, the Cyclopes, and the Hecatoncheires. Later, Uranus turned against his own family by placing them in the underworld of Tartarus, where Gaia was tormented for months in pain. Uranus hated the Cyclopes and the Hecatoncheires, placing them in chains in a dungeon in the underworld. In retaliation, Gaia used Cronus to plot against his father, Uranus, through castration. After Cronus castrated his father with a flint, he threw his father's testicles into the sea of Cyprus, where the blood from the testicles supernaturally gave rise to Venus, the goddess of love and beauty; and from the blood also arose the giants, who later became nemeses to the Olympian gods. Cronus then married his sister Rhea, who later gave birth to the Olympian Greek Gods: Zeus, Hestia, Demeter, Hera, Hades, and Poseidon. The Olympians were very humanlike, tall, beautiful, and athletic in appearance, in comparison to the Titans, who were very grotesque but possessed the same powers as the Olympian gods. Cronus was foretold by a prophecy that the Olympian gods would one day overthrow him. In resentment, Cronus ate his children one by one. When Rhea found out about Cronus's plot to destroy the Olympian gods, she became upset and hid Zeus, disguising him as a stone. Long after Zeus grew up, Rhea told Zeus the whole truth about his siblings; and Zeus sought advice from a Titan, Metis, in the underworld of Tartarus, who prepared a potion that would free the Olympian gods from Cronus's stomach. As Zeus disguised himself as a cupbearer, he gave the potion to his elderly father, Cronus, who soon vomited up all of Zeus's brothers and sisters. After the Olympian gods imprisoned Cronus for his bad behavior, the Titans were still on Cronus's side and went to war with the Olympian gods for ten years. Finding out that both sides were evenly matched, Zeus knew the only way to end the war was to free the Cyclopes and the Hecatoncheires, who hated Cronus. When the Cyclopes and the Hecatoncheires joined together with the Olympian gods in battle, the Olympian gods defeated the Titans, imprisoning them in the underworld of Tartarus. Revengefully, Gaia became angry at the Olympian gods for defeating her children and sent a ten-headed dragon, Typhoeus, against the Olympian gods, which captured Zeus. Later, Hermes freed Zeus, who then defeated the ten-headed dragon by striking it with lightning. In the last battle, the giants that rose up from Cronus's blood wanted to dethrone the Olympian gods' rule over Mount Olympus. Along with the help of the Olympian gods and Hercules, they vanquished the giants, using all their immortal powers and strength. Homer became the first Greek poet to create myths about the ancient gods during the Mycenaean Ages, and later Virgil became another famous poet in Rome. He took the original Olympian gods' names and translated them into Latin names.

Background of the major deities (gods, goddesses, titans, demigods, and heroes) and their Roman equivalent. Zeus (Jupiter) became the supreme leader over the Olympian gods after freeing his brothers and sisters from Cronus's stomach. Zeus's affairs with other women led to a great offspring of warriors like Hercules, Athena, and Apollo, who helped Zeus defeat the giants. Zeus is equivalent to the sky god, associated with lightning and thunder, and his symbol is the eagle.

Hera (Juno) is an original Olympian goddess, the protector of women's rights. She is the sister and wife of Zeus.

Poseidon (Neptune) is an original Olympian god and the ruler of the seas, also known as the earth shaker. Poseidon lost *a competition to Athena, and his anger resulted in a water shortage in Athens.*

Demeter (Ceres) is an original Olympian goddess of vegetation. Zeus mated with his sister Demeter, giving birth to Persephone.

Hades (Pluto) is an original Olympian god and the ruler of the underworld, Tartarus. He kidnapped Persephone for a wife.

Hestia (Vesta) is an original Olympian Greek goddess of the hearth, representing family and peace.

Athena (Minerva) was born in full war armor out from Zeus's head. After winning a competition over Poseidon, Athena became the model patroness for Athens, as the goddess and protector. Her symbol is the olive plant, representing wisdom and peace.

Apollo (Phoebus) is the god of archery, plagues, healing, and prophecy and the offspring of Zeus and Leto. During the Trojan War, he sided with the Trojan army.

Artemis (Diana) is the goddess of the forest, known to be a great female hunter.

Persephone (Proserpina) is the queen of the underworld, daughter of Zeus and Demeter.

Aphrodite (Venus) is the goddess of love and beauty. She supernaturally rose from the sea, into an adult woman, from Uranus's blood.

Eros (Cupid) was formed from chaos and is the son of Aphrodite. He is a beautiful winged angel who made all life on earth come together through love, like the union between Gaia and Uranus, which created the Titans.

Metis is the Titan goddess of wisdom and the daughter of one of the Titan gods. Zeus mated with Metis, giving rise to Athena.

Alcmene is the wife of Amphitryon, the king of Tiryns. Zeus mated with Alcmene, who gave birth at the same time to Hercules and Amphitryon's son, Iphicles.

Leto is a Titan goddess who became pregnant with Apollo and Artemis after sleeping with Zeus. Hera, the jealous wife of Zeus, cursed Leto from giving birth to her two kids on any land. She eventually found the floating island Delos, where she was able to give birth to both of her kids.

Leda is the original wife of Tyndareus, the king of Sparta. Zeus, in the form of a swan, seduced Leda, giving birth to Helen.

Helen is a demigod, the offspring of Zeus and Leda. She is the most beloved woman in Greece for her beauty.

Hercules is the equivalent of the Celtic hero Cú Chulainn, known for his enormous strength to kill wild beasts and mortal men with his bare hands. Hercules is the offspring of Zeus and Alcmene.

Gaia is the primal goddess of Mother Earth, supernaturally giving rise to the sea gods and Uranus.

Uranus is the son and husband of Gaia. His personification is the sky god, who mated with Gaia, giving rise to the Titans.

Cronus is the son of Gaia and Uranus. Cronus came to power after castrating his father Uranus. Later, he mated with his sister Rhea, giving birth to the original Olympian gods.

Rhea is a Titan goddess and the wife of Cronus.

Achilles was a famous warrior known for his invincibility in warfare and the slaying of the great warrior Hector.

The Three Graces are beautiful sister goddesses representing beauty, charm, and grace. They are the offspring of Zeus and Eurynome.

Nymphs are beautiful human female deities found in nature.

Satyrs are represented as a half goat, half man that stands on two legs, with a goat's tail. They are lustful creatures, chasing after female nymphs in the woods.

Sphinxes are large winged monsters with a human head and a body of a lion.

Bacchus is the ritual god of wine, symbolizing celebration of life, love, and peace.

Helen of Troy

The fascination with Helen's beauty led many men to lust after her, resulting in their downfall and the start of the Trojan War. At a very young age, Helen was abducted by Theseus, a great king of Athens, and Pirithous of Sicily. Their plan was to stick together before they died and abduct two of Zeus's daughters to have sex with. After Theseus seduced Helen, he left her in the safekeeping of his mother, Aethra; and then both men went to the underworld, Tartarus, to seduce Persephone. As Theseus and Pirithous ventured into the underworld, Hades, the guardian of the underworld, knew their intentions and punished them both with eternity in prison in the underworld. After Helen was rescued by her brothers, Castor and Pollux, she returned to Sparta, where she was later offered in marriage by her father. Suitors from all over Greece had to take an oath that once Helen found a mate, they were liable to protect her if she was ever abducted again. Once Helen's father chose Menelaus as her husband, she was then abducted again by Paris of Troy, which led to the Trojan War. The *Iliad*, written by Homer, is credited with recounting the abduction of Helen during the Trojan War.

The Iliad

The *Iliad* is about a Trojan priest demanding the return of his daughter, Chryseis, from King Agamemnon, ruler of the Greeks. After King Agamemnon refuses to do so, Apollo sends a plague that decimates the Greek army. Realizing the loss of men, Agamemnon finally returns the priest's daughter; but in compensation, Achilles, the great warrior, has to give up his woman in place of Chryseis, which makes Achilles furious at King Agamemnon. After Achilles leaves the Greek army, the Greek forces start to falter without Achilles' presence; and then his best friend, Patroclus, is killed by the Trojans. After hearing the news about his best friend Patroclus being killed, Achilles becomes very vengeful and returns to the Greek army, defeating the Trojan forces. Throughout the book of the *Iliad*, Homer illustrated the gods fighting against one another during the Trojan War, with many poetic descriptions of the gods' appearances during battle, having golden-blond to reddish hair, with comb locks, brightly colored eyes of blue, hazel, or gray, and skin complexion that is pale white to rosy bright red, showing through their skin.

CHAPTER 4

Western Philosophy

Mathematical and Philosophical Beauty

History of the golden ratio

The Egyptians were the first Babylonians to use the golden ratio in there architectural designs—from the pyramids, statues, paintings, and pottery. Later on, Thales became the first Greek philosopher to learn math from the Egyptians. He applied his mathematical knowledge into finding the height of pyramids, distance of ships off the seashore, and the Thales's theorem. Pythagoras became a follower of Thales, applying his own mathematical theories, stating that all things were from numbers—from the plants, animals, humans, musical instruments, pyramids—and were created in their form of aesthetics in relation to the golden ratio. Based on Pythagoras's knowledge of numbers, he transformed the minds of many philosophers, sculptures, painters, and architectures into designing their architectural work into proportional perfection. The Pythagorean theorem helped to prove his theory on mathematical beauty. The golden ratio is defined as the smaller length is in perfect proportion to the longer length—length a/b= 1/2 or 1.618.

Examples of the golden ratio in nature

The human form is a perfect model for the golden ratio. In illustration 1 below, when dividing the human body horizontally into two sections, the feet to the navel in is longer than from the navel to the top of the head. The foundation always has to be stronger and support more weight in which the legs are the largest and strongest muscles in the body, supporting the smaller body parts of the upper body. If the feet to the navel was the same length as the navel to the top of the head, then it won't be called a golden ratio because it would be proportionally off balance, with the same weight on the top as it is at the bottom. Fibonacci was a mathematician who founded the Fibonacci principle.

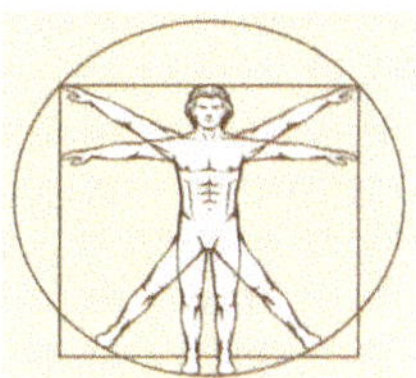

Illustration 1

The Fibonacci principle is a sequence of numbers found most commonly in nature, and the pattern starts off as 1, 2, 3, 5, 8, 13, 21, 34, 55, 89, 144. Fibonacci created this number sequence by starting the number sequence off with 1, 2, which is part of the golden ratio; and by adding the first two numbers in sequence, you get the third pattern number, then so on. Examples of the Fibonacci principle can be seen in a rose, a daisy, a pine cone, and a nautilus shell in illustration 2 below.

Illustration 2

Triangle—the pyramids

The pyramids were a main a burial place for the tombs of the pharaoh gods. The pyramids also helped with mathematicians—such as Thales, Pythagoras, Euclid—to correlate that the triangle shape is the most useful, solid, versatile geometric shape used into finding distances, area, lengths in other objects, and a model of proportional perfection. For example, when taking an isosceles triangle and making seven other triangles inside it, you could draw a circular line from the smaller one up to the other big corresponding triangles, creating a perfect golden spiral.

Mathematical beauty of the triangle

Mathematical beauty can be found in the Pythagorean theorem, as well as other shapes that present the golden triangle, such as the isosceles triangle in illustration 3 below—golden rhombus, golden rectangle, and pentagram.

Golden triangle

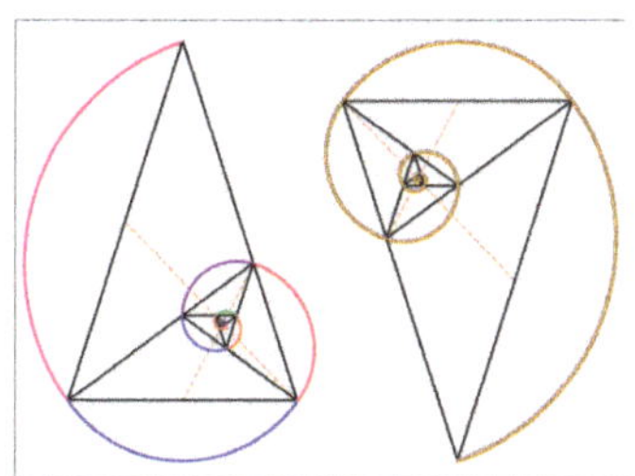

Illustration 3. Isosceles Triangle

Golden ratio in architectural designs

Many architectural designs that represent the golden ratio are ones like the Parthenon temple, the statue of Polykleitos, and the *Mona Lisa* painting.

Marquardt beauty mask

The Marquardt beauty mask was invented in 1960 by an American dentist named Stephen R. Marquardt. He founded a relationship among people with narrow shaped faces as attractive and then compared them to the shape of a square, which is the representation to the beauty mask of the golden ratio.

Mathematical and structural beauty quotes

Polykleitos. Polykleitos quoted that "beauty consists in the proportion, not of the elements [materials] but of the parts that is the interrelation of parts with one another and with the whole."

*Vitruvius.*_Vitruvius is famous for asserting in his book *De Architectura* that "a structure must exhibit the three qualities of *firmitas, utilitas, venustas*—that is it must be solid, useful, beautiful."

Aristotle. Aristotle quoted, "The chief forms of beauty are order and symmetry and definiteness which the mathematical sciences demonstrate in a special degree."

History of Western philosophers on beauty

After the fall of the Roman Catholic church, a new class of wealthy citizens began to flourish in Florence, Italy, inspiring painters and philosophers to take the center stage. During the Renaissance period, painters like Botticelli, da Vinci, Raphael, and Michelangelo painted many of their characters in their secular form of beauty in accordance to the golden ratio, making their images appear larger and as the center of attraction. Paintings like the *Mona Lisa* painting and *Ginevra de' Benci* were all popular paintings that contained the golden ratio. Even in the Renaissance period, many artists painted portraits for wealthy families, pertaining to their young daughters to signify their moral goodness to young men in marriage in order to win a man's heart through marriage, and as moral goodness, your physical appearance had to be made beautiful. This philosophical theme on physical beauty was philosophized throughout Westernization period until the mid-nineteenth century, where Westernization ended.

A brief history of Westernization

Westernization is when the European settlers went into other countries and influenced their beliefs on other cultures. During 400 BC, Alexander the Great became the first Western to spread Western art from Europe unto the Persian Empire and to Asia Minor. Then in AD 1492, Christopher Columbus discovered America, spreading European philosophies. Between 1856 and 1912, imperialism was a new form of Westernization. It was defined as another country coming into another continent and completely taking it over for economic and political status in efforts to help countries like Africa, Asia, and the Middle East become more civilized.

Western philosophers' ideas on physical beauty

Leonardo da Vinci quoted in his paintings, "Beauty de virtue"—meaning, in order to be of good character and moral goodness, your outer appearance had to appear or be made beautiful.

Michelangelo quoted, "The skin is more beautiful than the garment."

Raphael quoted, "Time is a vindictive bandit to steal the beauty of our former selves."

Robert Boyle quoted, "Beauty was not measured so much in colour of the skin but in stature, comely symmetry of the parts of the body, and good features in the face."

CHAPTER 5

Greek and Roman Architecture

Vitruvius knew that the human form was designed by nature and observed that the ancient Greeks used the human form as a guide into constructing the temples. In order for the Greeks to construct the temples in perfect proportions, they had to observe the physiques of well-shaped men—meaning, the ancient gods in Greece who were deemed for their beautiful, athletic appearance such as the statue Apollo Belvedere and Diana were all models of proportional perfection. Many of the ancient temples named after their gods or goddesses in Greece helped shaped the three main architectural orders, which were the Doric, Ionic, and Corinthian (illustration 2). The architectural orders were used to either support the weight of the abacus or used for decoration purposes in coliseums to theaters. In detail, the architectural orders are columns made out of white marble used to represent the aesthetics appeal of the gods. The top of the column is in representation to the capital—meaning the head and the shaft representing the body and the base representing the feet, in comparison to the caryatid (illustration 1).

Illustration 1

Doric order

The Doric order originated in 700 BC and was designed by Dorus or Ictinus and Callicrates. Vitruvius described the Doric order as the most commonly used in temples in Greece. The shaft is stockier in comparison to a man's build. It holds more weight than the Iconic and Corinthian orders.

Iconic order

The Iconic order originated in 6 BC, was designed by the Ionian Greeks, and was founded in the Ionian Islands. Vitruvius described the Iconic order as the most commonly used in smaller buildings; therefore, it holds less weight. The Iconic order was described to be slender in from in comparison to a women's build. The volutes on the Iconic form represents women's fallopian tubes.

Corinthian order

The Corinthian order originated in 500 BC, was designed by Callimachus, and was founded in the city of Corinthians. Vitruvius described the Corinthian order more like a young girl holding less weight, slender than the Iconic order. Vitruvius described the ornate curly acanthus leaves caping down from a Voltaire vase, mainly for decoration purposes.

Tuscan order

The Tuscan order originated around the Italian Renaissance period between AD 1550 and 1552 and was designed by Vignola Regola, Sebastiano Serlio, and Andrea Palladio. The Tuscan order is similar to the Doric order but is much plainer with no flutes along the column.

Composite order

The Composite order originated around the Italian Renaissance period between AD 1550 and 1552 and was designed by Vignola Regola, Sebastiano Serlio, and Andrea Palladio. The Composite order is a blend of the Iconic order and the Corinthian Order, representing the volutes around the capital together with the acanthus leaves.

CHAPTER 6

Greek and Roman Sculpture

Sculptures

The Classical period became the main focal point of humanism, representing the human form as a model of proportional perfection and youthful beauty. Many of the statues from the Classical period, up until the nineteenth century, are depicted as Aryan models, which are tall, athletic, and with blond hair. Throughout this chapter, you can see how the ancient Greeks and Romans place their emphasis on physical beauty, idolizing the Aryan gods as powerful mortals in a canon of perfection, expressing the harmony of the human form in various athletic positions.

Kouros

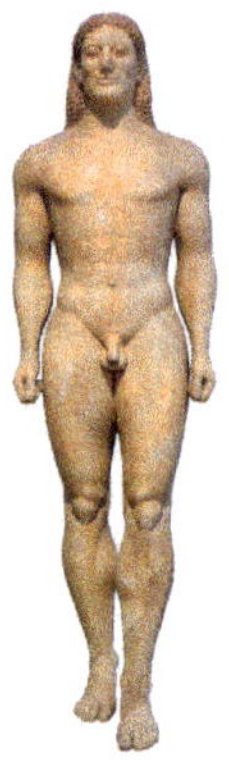

Majority of Greek artists adopted their methods from the Egyptian culture, who idolized their gods in skirted clothing, in paintings, or in statue form, such as Pharoah, Cleopatra, and King Tut. In contrary, the Greeks wanted to sculpt their gods in nude form to show them being beautiful and heroic. The standard Kouros stood with his left foot forward, arms at his sides, looking straight ahead. The sculpturer is still unknown, and this was created around 600 BC.

Kristos Boy

The statue Kristos Boy was named after its creator Kristos and was created in 480 BC. After, the Archaic period ended in Greece, the Greeks became knowledgeable of how the human body harmoniously worked together while in symmetrical positions. Observing the contrapposto of the body, you see the right leg is bent forward while all the weight is on the left leg, being straight, and the head is slightly turned to the right.

Discobolus

Myron was the first artist to express perfect harmony, balance, and proportion to the human form in motion. The statue Discobolus shows the ideal athlete throwing a disc in perfect alignment with the rest of his body. The sculpture was created in 450 BC.

Athena

The sculpture was created by Cephisodotus or Euphranor in 400 BC. This statue is a depiction of Athena, who's known to be the goddess, protector, and patron of Athens, Greece.

Apollo Belvedere

The sculpture was created by Leochares and was created in 360 BC. Apollo is known to be the god of music, archery, and prophecy and is shown releasing an arrow at one of his adversaries. The statue of Apollo Belvedere shows off his masculine beauty. In detail, he is seen wearing a cape around his body, with a quiver that suspends from his back and the display of his lightly curly hair flowing from his head to his neck.

Aphrodite of Cnidus

The sculpture was created by Praxiteles in 370 BC Aphrodite is known to be the Greek goddess of love, beauty, and sexuality—the equivalent to the Roman goddess Venus. Aphrodite of Cnidus is known to be the first female nude statue that exhibits female beauty and is shown Aphrodite bathing herself.

Laocoön and his sons

The sculpture was created by Polydorus Rhodes, Athendorous of Rhodes, and Agesander of Rhodes in 200 BC During the Trojan War, Laocoön was known as a Trojan priest who warned the people from messing with the wooden horse outside the City of Troy because it was sacred to the gods Apollo, Athena, and Poseidon. In suspicion, Laocoön himself, the priest, became tempted in messing with the wooden horse; he threw a spear at the horse, which resulted in punishment from the gods, sending sea serpents that killed Laocoön and his sons.

Zeus (Jupiter of Smyrna)

The sculpture is unknown and was created around AD 250. This statue is a depiction of Zeus. In Zeus's right hand is a thunderbolt; it was his main weapon to destroy those who came against him or disobeyed him.

David

This sculpture was created by Michelangelo in 1475. This is a depiction of the biblical character David in the Bible. David shown here is getting ready to go to battle against the evil giant Philistine warrior Goliath, who has challenged the Israelites into battle that would decide their fate, and David was the chosen one to go up against the giant. This sculpture by Michelangelo depicts David looking over at his shoulder at Goliath with full concentration, a sling on his left shoulder, and a stone in his right hand. The contrapposto of the statue David was to show the beautiful form of the human anatomy that was created in the early Renaissance.

Apollo and Daphne

This sculpture was created by Gian Lorenzo Bernini in 1598. This story is about a great warrior named Apollo, who mocked Cupid for being too childish to handle a weapon. In retaliation, the winged cupid Eros becomes upset, creating two arrows—one to love someone, the other arrow to loath a person—shooting them both at Apollo and Daphne. When Apollo falls in love with Daphne, she refuses his every plea, loathing him, pleading with her father, Perius, to turn her into a tree, refraining any man from falling in love with her or lusting after her. Long after Daphne is turned into a tree, Apollo never gives up loving her, standing right by her side day and night, guarding, protecting her from any wild beast trying to harm her.

The Rape of Persephone

The sculpture was created by Gian Lorenzo Bernini in 1621. One day, Persephone was outside picking flowers when Pluto from the underworld kidnaps Persephone for a wife. Her mother, Demeter, pleads with Zeus, her father, to get Persephone back and makes a deal with Pluto to release her only if Persephone doesn't eat anything while in the underworld. Somehow, Persephone got tempted and ate pomegranate seeds, which delayed her being released from the underworld. The statue depicts Pluto raping Persephone and the anguish that is on Persephone's face as the tears are pouring down her face, resisting Pluto from ravishing her.

Borghese as Venus

The sculpture was created by Antonio Canovas Paolina in 1757. The story of the judgment of Paris is about a wedding where Eris, the goddess of discord, was not allowed to attend because her presence will cause strife among people. So, in outrage of not being invited to the wedding, she threw the apple of discord into the wedding ceremony where the three goddesses Hera, Aphrodite, and Athena all claimed the apple at the same time. The golden apple addressed to the fairest—meaning, the prize of beauty—and in order for the three to claim the prize, they had to settle the dispute among a judge named Paris, a Trojan mortal. Upon arrival, the three goddesses tried to bribe the judge in order to gain favor, but Venus eventually won his approval by promising him to get Helen, the world's most beautiful woman, who soon brought on the Trojan War.

Cupid and Psyche

The sculpture was created by Antonio Canovas in 1787. The story called *The Golden Ass* is about Psyche, an ordinary young woman being loved by the people in her town for her remarkable beauty but is envied by the goddess Venus. So, one night, Venus sends her son, Cupid, a winged angel, on an errand to place a spell over Psyche that will confuse her into marrying someone physically unattractive, but instead, Cupid ditches the plan, making himself fall in love with Psyche. Long after, Psyche finds out what happens. She then redeems herself to Venus by doing different task for her, and the final task was to retrieve a dose of beauty in the underworld in order for Venus to retain her beauty back after attaining to her ailing son. After Psyche attains the dose of beauty in the underworld, she walks out of the cave and becomes curious, opening the dose of beauty where she falls into a deep sleep. As Psyche begins to awake in Cupid's arms, Cupid immediately pricks Psyche with an arrow, and immediately, Psyche falls in love with Cupid.

Diana

The sculpture was created in 1848 by Augustus Saint-Gaudens. Diana was a goddess, equivalent to goddess Artemis, who can skillfully hunt, kill, and control wild animals. Augustus Gaudens sculpted

Diana as the idealist for perfect feminine beauty. Looking at her slender figure, you can see Diana's face in complete composure as she stands on her left foot, aiming her bow and arrow in perfect counterbalance with the rest of her body in motion.

The Rape of Polyxena

The sculpture was created in 1865 by Pio Fedi. During the Trojan War, Polyxena makes a vow to Achilles promising him marriage if the Greek army stops besieging the City of Troy. In contrary, Polyxena betrays Achilles by having her brothers kill Achilles with an arrow in his foot. In revenge, Achilles comes back as a ghost, promising to kill Polyxena for betraying him, and in this sculpture, you can see Achilles raping Polyxena while raising his sword toward Polyxena's mother, Hecuba. Hecuba is seen holding on to Achilles' leg, pleading to Achilles not to kill her daughter.

Psyche/Berufung

Between 1933 and 1942, Arno Breker was a German sculpture who was commissioned by Hitler and the Nazi Party to propagate that the Aryan race were superior to all others. Many of Breker's sculptures were made from viewing actual human models that portrayed the Aryan race as athletic and beautiful.

CHAPTER 7

Roman Painters

Painters

After the fall of the Roman Catholic church, many Florentine artists in the Renaissance readopted humanism back into their art, representing characters from the mythological world. During the Renaissance period, Ovid became famous for his popular poem called the *Metamorphoses*, a poem made up of fifteen sections, talks about the mythological gods falling in love and that the challenges they face is similar to human emotions. Not only was the *Metamorphoses* the most popular book in the Renaissance but it helped inspire painters from the Renaissance period unto the neoclassical period, depicting their characters in secular form of beauty, representing them as deities higher than mankind.

Ginevra de' Benci

The Leonardo da Vinci created this portrait in 1474. During the Renaissance, many artists painted portraits for wealthy families, pertaining to their young daughters, to signify that in order to win a man's heart through marriage, your physical appearance had to be made beautiful or appear beautiful, which is a sign of moral goodness. This meaning on physical beauty is similar to the inscription Leonardo wrote below the portrait of the Ginevra de Benci, quoting, "VIRTVTEM FORMA DECORAT,"—meaning, "beauty adorns virtue." This portrait was to honor her marriage to Luigi de Bernardo Niccolini at the age of sixteen.

The Primavera

The painting was created in 1482 by Sandro Botticelli. This painting was commissioned by the Medici family and was hung in the bedroom for one of the brides. Botticelli referred to certain mythological figures of love and fertility—that during marriage comes love; when love advances, sex comes, which produces human offspring. Similar to the meaning behind *spring*, it means a time of new growth, a rebirth of new things. From a long winter, flowers begin to grow, as well as plants grow to their full potential. In this painting contains nine mythological figures. Venus is in the center; she is the main figure that represents sexual desire and marriage. Above Venus is a blindfolded Cupid. To the left are three women in sheer clothing, holding hands. They are the Three Graces. To the far left is Mercury; he is a guy dressed in a red cloak with a sword by his waist, showing him reaching up with a stick to usher away the winter clouds. To the very far right is Zephyrus, the wind god, a bluish figure who is seen grabbing a woman named Chloris. The scene in this painting is in a grove where oranges, and flowers are plentiful.

Mars and Venus

The painting was created by Sandro Botticelli in 1483. This painting shows the two Roman gods Mars and Venus as lovers leisurely in the forest after making love to each other. On the right shows Mars lying naked on a red cloak with a white sheet over him, and Venus is shown to the left, gazing at her lover, while the four satyrs are playing with his war armor. The hornet seen buzzing over Mars resembles stings of love. The allegory of this painting is love, and through intimate love comes compassion for one another.

The Birth of Venus

The painting was created by Sandro Botticelli in 1485. The birth of Venus came about when Gaia, the mother goddess, demanded Uranus to be punished for the anguish he caused both her and children in the underworld of Tartarus. Cronus, one of Gaia's sons, was brave enough to take out Gaia's demands using a flint to castrate his father, Uranus. From the blood of the testicles gave rise to Venus, the naked woman standing up on a shell. Venus was guided to shore by the two winged angels Zephyrus and Chloris. To the far right, Pomona, known as the goddess of spring, awaits Venus to cloth her naked body with a floral cloak.

Mona Lisa

The *Mona Lisa* painting is one of the most famous works by Leonardo da Vinci and was created in 1503. In this portrait shows Mona posing centered to proportional perfection in the portrait. Her beautiful pale skin offsets the misty landscape in the background, along with her starring gaze and smile.

The Three Graces

The painting was created by Raphael in 1504. The *Three Graces* are three sister goddesses that represent charm, grace, beauty, and fertility. This painting by Raphael shows the transitions of womanhood: on the far left represents the maiden (chastitas)—meaning, virgin—seen wearing a girded skirt, and the woman on the far right is maturity (voluptuous)—meaning, she has grown into an adult woman—seen wearing a necklace. The apples seen in the painting represent the golden apple from the garden of Hesperides—meaning, the apple of discord used to signify the starting of an argument could lead to a bigger dispute.

The Creation of Man

The painting was created Michelangelo in 1511. This panting is about how God created mankind through Adam and how Eve came about when God reached toward Adam to pull a rib from him. Eve is shown to the far right; under God's shoulder, you see a woman. God is shown on the right, as the large authoritative figure in a white cloak, and then to the left is Adam in nude form. In detail, it shows the beautiful athletic form of God is similar to that of Adam and to know that God created Adam in his own image.

Separation of Light from Darkness

This painting was created by Michelangelo in 1512. This painting is from the perspective of the book of Genesis. In the center of the painting, it depicts God rising into the sky with arms outstretched, separating the light from darkness, and in the four corners of the painting shows the beauty of the four male nudes.

The Cherubs (Sistine Madonna)

This painting was created by Raphael in 1512. For centuries, the winged cherubs became famous for their conspicuous gaze and appear to have Nordic features.

Titian's Venus and Adonis

This painting was created by Tiziano Vecellio in 1553. This painting shows Venus holding on to her lover, Adonis, sensing that Adonis will die while hunting. Venus is known for her beauty, but it shows Adonis's love for hunting is more desirable than Venus. Other descriptions in this painting show signs of dark clouds in the background, depicting the gloom and doom that will lead to Adonis's death.

Atlantia and Hippomenes

This painting was created by Guido Reni in 1622. Atlantia was a great female hunter, not only known for her great hunting ability but also for her beauty. Disliking the idea of marriage, Atlantia decided to marry only if her male companion outraced her, and if they failed to do so, they would be put to death. Hippomenes, the lover, is shown on the far right lunging forward, outracing Atlantia while throwing apples at her. The apples before the race were given to Hippomenes by Venus, promising him to win the race if he threw it at Atlantia, distracting her.

Peace and War

Peter Paul Rubens was a painter from Spain. He created this painting in 1630. He was sent to England as a diplomatic post to King Charles of England to create *Peace and War*, a finished work as an offering in order to stop the onset of war amongst the two nations. In the center of the painting represents a naked woman named Pax, the goddess of peace. She is shown giving milk to the infant Plutus, the god of wealth. The group of children on the right are portraits of Rubens's children; they represent the children of the future of mankind. Above the children is Minerva, a soldier with a shield, protecting the children from Mars, the god of war, who is seen looking back with a face of anguish as well as Alecto, the god of fury, looking back too. The winged cupid on the far right helps lead the fruit from the satyr to the children. Hymen is the goddess of marriage with the torch in her hand; she places a wreath on one of the children's head. To the far left are two naked women—one has a tambourine, and the other one is carrying a basket full of jewels, signifying the celebration of life and good spirits.

Jupiter and Antiope

This painting was created by Antoine Watteau in 1714. This artwork shows two main figures—Jupiter, who is the brownish satyr, is seen looking upon the sleeping princess Antiope. The scene here, shows the satyr sneaking upon her, gazing at her, lustfully licking his lips, getting ready to ravish her.

The Toilet of Venus

This painting was created by Francois Boucher in 1751. Madame de Pompadour was well known for her political status and wealth and helped Francois commissioned many of his paintings to success. This scene here was painted in the actual bedroom of Madame de Pompadour. The allusion depicts Madame de Pompadour as the goddess of Venus. You can see the little winged angels floating around Venus, representing Venus as a symbol of love and beauty. Surrounding her bed is an overflow of dazzling jewels, satins, and silks. This shows the enormous wealth of Madame de Pompadour.

Morpheus and Iris

This painting was created by Pierre-Narcisse Guérin in 1811. Morpheus is known to be the god of sleep—meaning, he could appear in anyone's dream in any shape or form, such as a human, animal, or insect. This painting is a depiction of the sleeping god Morpheus asleep while lying naked on white sheets, and Iris, who is the naked women appearing from the clouds, is getting ready to send Morpheus on an errand to deliver messages in someone's dream.

La Grande Odalisque

This painting was created by Jean Auguste Dominique Ingres in 1814. In real life, this painting was a display of Napoleon's sister, Caroline Murat, that was commissioned by herself and the queen of Naples. Jean Ingres's emphasis on the female form was to beautify it. He added an extra vertebra in order to provide perfect elongation of the backside that runs along the spine of the neck to the buttocks area. This is to emphasize the full curvature of the female backside.

Oedipus and the Sphinx

This painting was painted by Gustave Moreau in 1864. The two main figures in this painting are Oedipus, shown on the right with a red cloak, holding on to a stick; and to the left of Oedipus is the sphinx, a half-human–half-animal with eagle wings. This scene takes place in Thebes, on a rocky passage where travelers come through. Each traveler who passes the sphinx has to answer a riddle, and if they don't answer the riddle correctly, they will dissolve into human bones, as you can see the remnants of a skeleton foot on the ground. As you see, Oedipus is thinking really hard and soon answers the riddle correctly, winning the kingdom of Thebes.

Nymphs and Satyr

This painting was created by William-Adolphe Bouguereau in 1873. This painting shows a wooded area where three female nymphs are playfully trying to drag the satyr into the pond. In detail, you can see the satyr trying to resist against the female nymphs, with his hooves onto the ground; and you see the fourth nymph waving her hand, gesturing to a group of nymphs in the far right background to come join in on the fun. Bouguereau placed emphasis on female body, showing the different views of the four nymphs in the painting.

CHAPTER 8

Racial Superiority

Scientific racism

From 1880 to 1914, Darwin was a major pioneer in shaping racial superiority in Europe when other European countries such as Britain, France, Spain, and Germany went into developing countries and adopted their own theories of racial anthropology. Racial anthropology helps classify individuals of each different ethnic group—comparing skeleton makeup, brain capacity, and IQs to correlate that Europeans are a much superior stock than other races in intellect and outward beauty. Scientific racism not only helped shaped racial superiority but the eugenics movement as well. The eugenics movement was founded by Francis Galton, the cousin of Darwin. The eugenics movement is a movement based on selective breeding programs in order to exterminate the undesired traits of certain individuals in which the movement transpired into exterminating and sterilizing the inferior races such as the Jews, Blacks, and Gypsies in order to keep the genetic bloodline of the White race pure.

On the Origin of Species

Darwin stated in his book *On the Origin of Species* that "all distinct races of mankind derived from Africa." Evidently, based on archeologist findings, the first humans to evolve was of a skeleton of a Neanderthal, which is similar to an ape in Africa. Darwin believed that the first humans to walked on all four limbs adapted to its environment and started walking upright. Darwin also knew the body can adapt to new things over time, just like babies who are curious in their surrounding environments—they begin to touch things and learn to walk, talk, and reason, and their brain cells begin to grow.

Darwin theorized that based on technological advancement of Whites, compared to aboriginals—Blacks today—he believed that Whites are far more superior to the darker races because, based on scientific racism, Darwin believed that Black brains were smaller than Whites based on the cranial size of their skull. In addition, the primitive features of Blacks retained animalistic characteristics of an ape. This reasoning led Darwin to believe that Blacks in Africa and Australia didn't have the brains to progress into a more advance civilization but had more of the primitive characteristics of the Neanderthal, like hunting and living out of huts, into the nineteenth century in illustration 1 below.

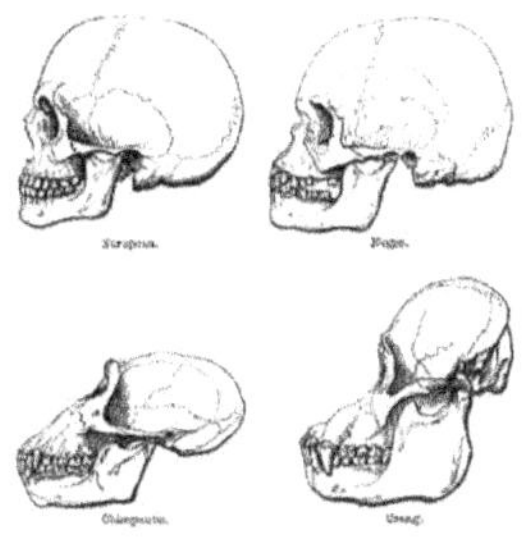

Illustration 1. Classifying skull types

Natural selection

Based on natural selection, Darwin theorized that during the primitive stages of mankind, he believed that Whites overpowered the Blacks in the fight for land, racial domination, and hierarchy. Due to the larger brain capacity of Whites, they were far more intelligent to create advanced weaponry in order to create slaves out of them. In survival of the fittest, more Whites overpowered the Blacks, either colonizing their land or exterminating them in order for the strongest to survive.

Darwinian influence

Darwin helped inspire anthropologists and biologists to adopt his method on human evolution of how each distinctive race is different based on the adaption to their environment. Hitler believed Darwin's ideology, then adopted his own theories in the book called the *Mein Kampf*, stating differently that Whites are a separate and superior bloodline from the garden of Eden in heaven compared to the subhuman races, like the Jews and Blacks.

CHAPTER 9

The Master Race

Darwin's ideology on race has inspired Hitler to believe the Aryan race was a far more superior in intelligence than to the subhuman races on earth. In the book called *On the Origin of Species*, Darwin stated that based on smaller brain capacity of Blacks, they didn't have the brains to progress into a more advance civilization than Whites but still had more of the primitive characteristics like living out of a hut, hunting for food into the nineteenth century.

In comparison to Whites, Darwin theorized that during the primitive stages of mankind, he believed that Whites, through natural selection, overpowered the Blacks in the fight for land, racial domination, and hierarchy. Due to the larger brain capacity of Whites, they were far more intelligent to create advanced weaponry in order to create slaves out of them. Notable Aryans such as Alexander the Great and Augustus were noble conquerors who conquered vast empires from Europe to Asia Minor, where lots of cultures were forced to adopt the Western ideas of the Roman culture. In addition, Thales was the first Aryan mathematician to influence many Greek philosophers, scientists, and architects into the development of the many great technologies you see today in the Western world from bridges to roads, buildings, aqueducts, central air-conditioning, etc. According to the book *Mein Kemp*, Hitler used the term *master race* to define the Aryan race as superior to all others, creating laws forbidding other races such as the Jews, Blacks, or Gypsies from intermixing with the good genes of the Aryan race. If either Jew or Aryan White person was ever found together, it was a crime punishable by death. Throughout Europe, Hitler promoted the aesthetics appeal of the Aryan race on posters, billboards, and TV, portraying the blond hair–blue-eyed look were the standard of beauty in Europe (illustration 1). Then, during World War II, Nazi Germany helped inspire the aesthetics of the blond hair–blue-eyed appeal through many of their actresses, like Marlene Dietrich and Betty Grable, who played in a lot of German films, came to Hollywood, and became the blonde sex symbol of American films. Betty Grable became very popular in America, known for her mass production of the pinup girl model, as well as her beautiful million-dollar legs.

Illustation 1

CHAPTER 10

Standard of Beauty

During Westernization, many philosophers from Europe shaped their beliefs on physical beauty, stating that outer beauty is a representation of moral goodness, which transpired into the age of imperialism. In the age of imperialism, leaders of the scientific community like Charles Darwin, Francis Galton, and Benjamin Rush shaped White superiority in America, stating that Black skin was a disease and that Blacks were inferior to Whites in mind, body, and intelligence, affecting the preconception of Blacks around the world, viewing them as inferior to White people. Over time, Hollywood accepted these negative views on Black people as being savages, comparing them to the good side, pertaining to White superheroes, White actors, and White actresses. This misconception has brainwashed our society into accepting that White is right and Black is wrong, so we accepted whiteness as a form of purity, righteous, and excellence for every culture in our society to strive for. When looking back to the standard of beauty in Hollywood in the early nineteenth century, predominately White actors and actresses—such as Marlene Dietrich, Betty Grable, Grace Kelly, Marilyn Monroe, Clark Gable, and Marlon Brando—flooded the Hollywood screens and became the model of iconic beauty around the world for people to look up to (illustration 1). When Disney films were first introduced in the early 1930s, *Snow White and the Seven Dwarves* became a hit, then other Disney films followed like *Alice in Wonderland*, *Cinderella*, *Sleeping*

Beauty, *Beauty and the Beast*—all these movies represented the landscape of what princesses should look like as a role model for young girls who imitate at an early age. Also, the most commonly handsome superheroes that played roles for young boys are Superman, Hercules, He-man, Conan the Barbarian, Batman and Robin—all had the common Aryan look: tall, thin with a muscular tone, with a narrow-shaped face. In 1921, the first American beauty pageant was held at Atlantic City, New Jersey, boardwalk in order to attract tourist; and the one main qualification for the beauty pageant was that you had to be of European descent. In the English literature, some of the most popular books that were read in high school through college were books like *Romeo and Juliet*, *Les Miserables*, *Mice and Men*, *Illiad*, *Odyssey*, *Metamorphoses*, *Pride & Prejudice*—books talking about fair-skinned people being beautiful, which is biased to people of color, who reads them. In the 1960s, the Marquardt beauty mask was invented to show the common relationship among people that have Aryan features, representing their faces in comparison to the beauty mask.

Illustration 1

CHAPTER 11

The Effects of Westernization

Today in the twenty-first century, majority of our TV ads, billboards, and movies that are inundated with European dominance—thin, fair-skinned tall people—has psychologically affected the way we look at ourselves or treat people based on looks. When going to a shopping mall to shop for clothes, a dealership to purchase a car to buying a home, sometimes salespeople will go the extra mile in helping attractive customers receive the best deal versus the unattractive person because by human nature our eyes are the senses to our brains, triggering neurotransmitters called dopamine, which causes pleasure in our brains and released only when looking at someone that brings attraction to us.

More so, in this society we've been brainwashed to treat someone based on their looks than their inner character because Westernization has conditioned other cultures into believing that the White look is the predominately look of beauty or acceptance in our society; therefore, we give better treatment to those who are good-looking. On job interviews, the interviewer is looking for people with higher education, good communications skills, as well as good appearance, and to some degree, discrimination takes place when a person seems to be out of shape or disheveled because they think if you conduct yourself that way, you will perform the same way on the job, then more likely, you'll be turned down for the position. In school, young girls get teased about their weight, so in order to appease their friends, they will sometimes go to the extreme by starving themselves until they black out or come close to dying, which is a form of anorexia.

In our everyday lives, we sometimes get caught up in the world's standards on the way we should look. Whether it be a firmer body, high bridge nose, less wrinkles, six-pack abs, or broader chest, we are all influenced by the Western culture on TV or by what other people think about us in a negative way of not having a certain appeal of attraction. So, in order to build our self-esteem up, we tend to get plastic surgery to look more appealing or attractive. Particularly in the Eastern world today, the effects of Westernization has whitewashed other cultures into believing that European looks are the most desirable. When looking at the average movie actors or actresses, in the Eastern world, they appear to be much like the movie stars in Europe as well as America—narrow-shaped faces, thin, tall, fair-complexed with high bridge noses—which has psychologically affected many Easterners into thinking that fair skin is better.

And today, many countries like Nigeria, India, and China are turning to skin lightening creams that can make your skin appear lighter if applied to the skin. In retrospect, the more you appear fair-skinned, the more you'll be accepted in society in status and beauty. In China, Japan, and Korea, some Asians are going to the extreme of getting plastic surgeries done on their eyes to appear more larger and rounder, similar to European eyes. In Iran, a high rate of women get plastic surgeries done on their nose to get the high bridge look, just like the Hollywood movie stars in America. In Japan, the youth idolized American and European popular culture so much that they dye their hair blond, brown, or red in order to look fashionable (illustration 1). Esther Honig, a journalist who was curious about the standard of beauty around the world, had her face photoshopped in over twenty-five different countries.

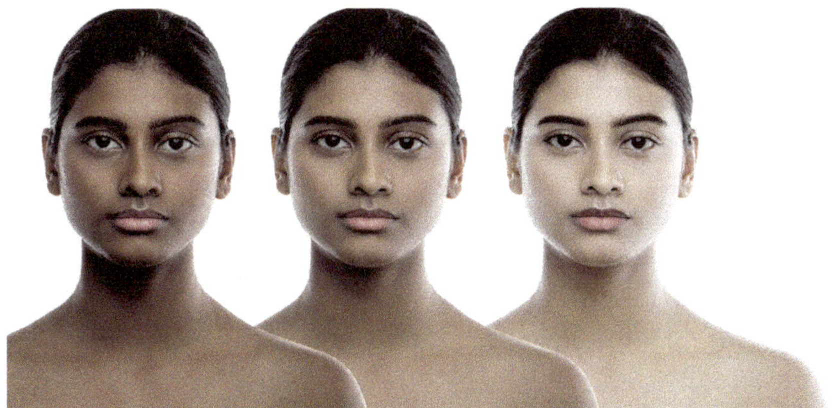

With skin whitening creams in India

WORKS CITED

Adhikari, Saugat. n.d. "Top Ten Outstanding Ancient Egyptian Paintings." Ancient History Lists. Accessed September 12, 2016. http://www.ancienthistorylists.com/egypt-history/Top-10-Outstanding-Ancient-Egyptian-Paintings.

Admin, Br. 2016. "Beauty Whitewashed: How White Ideals Exclude Women of Color." Beauty Redefined. Accessed September 12, 2016. http://www.beautyredefined.net/beauty-whitewashed-how-white-ideals-exclude-women-of-color.

Adow, Mohammed. 2013. "Nigeria's Danger." Al Jazeera. Accessed September 12, 2016. http://www.Aljazeera.com/indepth/features/2013/04/20134514845907984.html.

Agence France-Presse. 2015. "Ivory Coast Bans Potentially Deadly Skin-Whitening Creams." *The Guardian*. The Guardian News. Accessed September 12, 2016.

"Albinism." Wikipedia: The Free Encyclopedia. Wikimedia Foundation Inc. Accessed September 12, 2016. https://en.wikipedia.org/wiki/Albinism.

"Alexander the Great." Wikipedia: The Free Encyclopedia. Wikimedia Foundation Inc. Accessed October 1, 2016. https://en.wikipedia.org/Wiki/Alexander_The_Great.

Ancient Code. 2012. "Ancient Genetic Engineers: Ancient Texts Suggest Beings from Above Created Modern Man." Ancient Code. Accessed August 1, 2017. https://www.ancient-code.com/ancient-genetic-engineers-the-aliens-that-created-modern-man-according-to-ancient-texts/.

"Ancient Egyptian Religion." Wikipedia: The Free Encyclopedia. Wikimedia Foundation Inc. Accessed September 19, 2016. https://en.wikipedia.org/wiki/Ancient_Egyptian_Religion.

"Ancient Egyptian Technology." Wikipedia: The Free Encyclopedia. Wikimedia Foundation Inc. Accessed October 1, 2016. https://en.wikipedia.org/Wiki/Ancient_Egyptian_Technology.

"Ancient History." Pearson Education. Accessed September 12, 2016. http://www.infoplease.com/ipa/A0001198.html.

"The Ancient Race," "Giants of Eastern Asia," "China-Picture Heavy." Above Top Secret. The Above Network LLC. Accessed 2016. http://www.abovetopsecret.com/forum/Thread784614/pg1.

"The Annunaki: Enki and Enlil." Accessed August 3, 2017 https://groups.yahoo.com/neo/groups/SumerianStudies/conversations/messages/591.

"Anthropology." Wikipedia: The Free Encyclopedia. Wikimedia Foundation Inc. Accessed September 21, 2016. https://en.wikipedia.org/Wiki/Anthropology.

"Anti-Christian Policies in the Roman Empire." Wikipedia: The Free Encyclopedia. Wikimedia Foundation Inc. Accessed September 19, 2016. https://en.wikipedia.org/wiki/Persecution_Of_Christians_in_The_Roman_Empire.

"Aphrodite." Wikipedia: The Free Encyclopedia. Wikimedia Foundation Inc. Accessed September 21, 2016. https://en.wikipedia.org/Wiki/Aphrodite.

"Aphrodite of Cnidus." Wikipedia: The Free Encyclopedia. Wikimedia Foundation Inc. Accessed September 21, 2016. https://en.wikipedia.org/Wiki/Aphrodite_Of_Cnidus.

"Apollo." Wikipedia: The Free Encyclopedia. Wikimedia Foundation Inc. Accessed September 19, 2016. https://en.wikipedia.org/wiki/Apollo.

"Apollo Belvedere." Rome, Vatican Museums, Pius-Clementine Museum, Octagonal Court. http://ancientrome.ru/art/artworken/img.htm?id=1453.

"Apollo Belvedere." Wikipedia: The Free Encyclopedia. Wikimedia Foundation Inc. Accessed September 21, 2016. https://en.wikipedia.org/Wiki/Apollo_Belvedere.

"Apollo and Daphne." Wikipedia: The Free Encyclopedia. Wikimedia Foundation Inc. Accessed September 21, 2016. https://en.wikipedia.org/Wiki/Apollo and Daphne.

"Apple of Discord." Wikipedia: The Free Encyclopedia. Wikimedia Foundation Inc. Accessed September 21, 2016. https://en.wikipedia.org/Wiki/Apple_Of_Discord.

Apuleius, Lucius. "Cupid and Psyche." Last modified February 24, 2015. http://www.pitt.edu/~Dash/Cupid.html.

"The Archangel" (War in Heaven). The Book of Revelation. Http://www.sacred-texts.com/chr/tbr/tbr051.htm.

Architectural Orders. 2014. "Tuscan Order." YouTube. Accessed September 12, 2016.

Architectural Orders. 2014. "Composite Order." YouTube. Accessed September 12, 2016.

"Aristotle." Wikipedia: The Free Encyclopedia. Wikimedia Foundation Inc. Accessed September 21, 2016. https://en.wikiquote.org/Wiki/Aristotle.

"Arno Breker." Wikipedia: The Free Encyclopedia. Wikimedia Foundation Inc. Accessed September 21, 2016. https://en.wikipedia.org/Wiki/Arno_Breker.

"Aryan (Nordic Alpine) Aliens." http://aryannordicalpinealiens.blogspot.com.

"Aryanity: Forbidden Secrets of the Ancient Aryans, Aliens, and Nazis." Aryanity. Accessed September 12, 2016. http://Aryanity.com/Chp-4-The-Race-Of-Giants-2/.

"Aryan Race: Aryanism: Unity through Nobility." Aryanism. Accessed September 12, 2016. http://Aryanism.net/Culture/Aryan-Race/.

"Atalanta And Hippomenes." Web Gallery of Art. Accessed September 12, 2016. http://www.wga.Hu/html_M/R/Reni/1/Atalanta.html.

"Atlantean Gardens: The Blue-Eyed Buddha." Atlantean Gardens. Accessed September 12, 2016. http://atlanteangardens.blogspot.com/2014/05/The-Blue-Eyed-Buddha.html.
"Atlantean Gardens: Quetzalcoatl, Kukulkan, Viracocha, Votan, Gucumatz." Atlantean Gardens. Accessed September 12, 2016. http://atlanteangardens.blogspot.com/2014/05/Quetzalcoatl-Kukulkan-Viracocha-Votan.html.
"Atlantean Gardens: Where Did Blue Eyes Originated From?" Atlantean Gardens. Accessed September 12, 2016. http://atlanteangardens.blogspot.com/2014/04/where-did-blue-eyes-originate-from.html.
"Atlantis and Its Inhabitants the Original White Race?" Above Top Secrets. The Above Network LLC. http://www.abovetopsecret.com/forum/thread201869/pg1.
Atsma, A. "Theoi Greek Mythology." Theoi Project. Accessed September 12, 2016. http:/www.Theoi.com/Greek-Mythology/Giants.Html.
Avia. 2018. "Symbolic Meaning of Seasons." Whats-Your-Sign.com. Accessed September 12, 2016. http://www.whats-your-sign.com/symbolic-meaning-of-seasons.html.
"Augustus Propagandists: Virgil, Horace and Ovid." Study.com. Accessed September 12, 2016. http://Study.com/Academy/Lesson/Augustus-Propagandists-Virgil-Horace-And-Ovid.html.
"Beauty." Wikipedia: The Free Encyclopedia. Wikimedia Foundation Inc. Accessed September 12, 2016. https://en.wikipedia.org/wiki/Beauty.
"Beauty Whitewashed." Wikipedia: The Free Encyclopedia. Wikimedia Foundation Inc. Accessed September 12, 2016. https://en.wikipedia.org/wiki/Beauty_Whitewashed.
Beckett, Wendy. 1994. *The Story of Painting*. New York: DK.
"Bernini-Galleria Borghese: The Rape of Persephone." maItaly. WordPress. Last modified March 2, 2011. https://maitaly.wordpress.com/2011/03/02/Bernini-Galleria-Borghese-The-Rape-Of-Persephone.

"The Biblical Curse of White Skin." Godlike Productions. Last modified May 8, 2014. http://www.godlikeproductions.com/forum1/message2177988/Pg1.

"The Birth of Venus by Botticelli." Uffizi. Accessed 2016. http://www.uffizi.org/Artworks/The-Birth-Of-Venus-By-Sandro-Botticelli/.

"Blonde Sex Symbol: Betty Grable the Girl With the Million Dollar Legs HD." YouTube. Accessed September 12, 2016.

Boersema, D., and K. Middleton. 2012. *History of Western Philosophy: The Facts on File Guide to Philosophy.* New York: Facts on File Inc.

"Bloodlines of the Nephilim: A Biblical Study." Beginning and End. http://Beginningandend.com/Bloodlines-Of-The-Nephilium-A-Biblical-Study/.

"Blood Purity and Nazi Germany." The History Learning Site. Accessed September 12, 2016. http://www.Historylearningsite.co.uk/blood_Purity_Nazi_Germany.htm.

The Book. 1976. Wheaton, Illinois: Tyndale House Publishers. 292-667.

"Botticelli's Primavera." Italian Renaissance. Last modified 2015. http://www.Italianrenaissance.org/A-Closer-Look-Botticellis-Primavera/.

Peter Bowler. 1993. *Darwinism.* New York: Twayne Publishers. 67–71.

Bouchez, C. "Serotonin: 9 Questions and Answers" WebMD. Accessed September 12, 2016. http://www.webmed.com/Depression/Features/Serotonin.

Bourne, M. 2016. "The Math Behind the Beauty." InMath. Interactive Mathematics. Accessed September 12, 2016. http://www.intmath.com/Numbers/math-Of-Beauty.php.

Brainard, G. 1994. "Effects of Light on the Brain and Behavior." International Lighting in Controlled Environments Workshop. National Aeronautics and Space Administration. Accessed September 12, 2016.

Brown, Y. 2011. "Why I Believe Beyonce Is Betraying All Black and Asian Women." MailOnline. Associated Newspapers Ltd.

Accessed September 12, 2016. http://www.dailymail.co.uk/debate/article-1358119/Beyonce-Knowles-Why-I-Believe-Betraying-All-Black-And-Asian-Women.

Bulfinch, T. 1834. *Bulfinch's Mythology*. New York: Thomas Y. Crowell Company.

Burton, J. "Burton Beyond: The Nephilim and the Roots of Civilization." Burton Beyond. Accessed September 12, 2016. http://www.burtonbeyond.com/id46.html.

Bushak, L. 2014. "Seeing Pretty Faces Rewards the Brain: Is Perceiving Beauty All a Chemical Reaction?" Medical Daily. IBT Media Inc. Accessed September 19, 2016. http://www.medicaldaily.com/seeing-pretty-faces-rewards-brain-perceiving.

Butler, S. 2012. "The Discobolus." Hidden History. WordPress. Accessed September 12, 2016. http://hiddenhistory.co.uk/antiquities/the-olympics-in-ancient-art/.

C., Ali, Ryleigh R., and Andrew G. "The Canon of Polykleitos." Greek Art. PBworks. Accessed September 12, 2016. http://sasgreekart.pbworks.com/w/page/10150036/The%20Canon%20of%20Polykleitos

"Canova, Paolina Borghese as Venus Victrix." Web Gallery of Art. http://www.wga.hu/frames-e.html?/html/c/canova/2/3paolina.html.

"The Catholic Church in Europe: The Reformation, Renaissance and Reformation." Skwirk Online Education. Red Apple Education Ltd. Accessed September 12, 2016. http://www.skwirk.com/p-c_s-56_u-422_t-1108_c-4278/the-catholic-church-in-europe/qid/the-catholic-church-in-europe/renaissance-and-reformation/the-reform.

Carina. "Westernization of Beauty." Misrepresentation in the Media. Accessed July 21, 2014. http://sites.google.com/site/misrepresentationinthemedia/westernization-of-beauty.html.

"Charities." Wikipedia: The Free Encyclopedia. Wikimedia Foundation Inc. Accessed September 21, 2016. https://en.wikipedia.org/wiki/charities.

"Charles Darwin." Wikipedia: The Free Encyclopedia. Wikimedia Foundation Inc. Accessed September 21, 2016. https://en.wikipedia.org/Wiki/Charles_Darwin.

Charles, R. H. "Noah: The Birth of Noah; The Book of Enoch." http://www.sacred-texts.com/jud/loj/loj106.htm.

"Christopher Columbus Discovers America, 1492." Eye Witness to History. Ibis Communications Inc. Accessed October 1, 2016. http://www.eyewitnesstohistory.com/columbus.htm.

"Classical Order." Wikipedia: The Free Encyclopedia. Wikimedia Foundation Inc. Accessed September 21, 2016. https://en.wikipedia.org/wiki/classical_order.

"Classical Orders in Architecture." Designing Buildings Wiki. Designing Buildings Ltd. Accessed September 12, 2016. http://www.Designingbuildings.co.uk/wiki/Classical_Orders_In_Architecture.

Craven, J. 2016. "What is Neoclassical Architecture." About. About Inc. Accessed September 12, 2016. http://architecture.about.com/od/neoclassical/a/what-is-neoclassical-architecture.htm

CNN. 2016. "Subconscious Racial Bias in Children." YouTube. Accessed September 12, 2016.

Colavito, J. 2015. "The Weirdly Anti-Semitic and Racist Claims Behind This Clickbait Article Will Shock You!" Jason Colavito. Accessed August 3, 2017. http://www.jasoncolavito.com/blog/the-weirdly-anti-semitic-and-racist-claims-behind-this-click-bait-article-will-shock-you.

"Composite Order." Wikipedia: The Free Encyclopedia. Wikimedia Foundation Inc. Accessed September 21, 2016. https://en.wikipedia.org/wiki/composite_order.

"Course XXIII: History of Man." http://www.santiagobovisio.com/ing/books/course23.htm.

Creswell, D. 2013/ "The Beauty of Satan: If I Were the Devil." WordPress. Accessed September 12, 2016. http://darrellcreswell.wordpress.com/2013/01/13/the-beauty-of-satan-if-i-were-the-devil-bible-verses.

"Cupid and Psyche" Wikipedia: The Free Encyclopedia. Wikimedia Foundation Inc. Accessed September 21, 2016.

"The Creation of Adam." Wikipedia: The Free Encyclopedia. Wikimedia Foundation Inc. Accessed October 1, 2016. https://en.wikipedia.org/wiki/the_creation_of_adam.

"Cupid and Psyche." Wikipedia: The Free Encyclopedia. Wikimedia Foundation Inc. Accessed September 21, 2016. https://en.wikipedia.org/wiki/cupid_and_psyche.

"Cycladic Art." Wikipedia: The Free Encyclopedia. Wikimedia Foundation Inc. Accessed September 19, 2016. https://en.wikipedia.org/wiki/Cycladic_Art.

"David (Michelangelo)." Wikipedia: The Free Encyclopedia. Wikimedia Foundation Inc. Accessed September 21, 2016. https://en.wikipedia.org/wiki/david_(michelangelo).

Das, S. 2018. "Bindi: The Great Indian Forehead Art." About.com. About Inc. Accessed September 12, 2016. http://Hinduism.about.com/od/bindis/a/bindi.htm.

"The Devil, Satan." http://www.pacinst.com/efh/chapter2/Satan.html.

Dewey, P. "Learn Basic Bible Timeline." Jesus Is Savior. Accessed September 12, 2016. http://www.jesus-is-savior.com/believer's%20corner/bible_timeline.htm.

"Diana." Heilbrunn Timeline of Art History. The Metropolitan Museum of Art. September 12, 2016. http://wwww.metmuseum.org/toah/works-of-art/28.101/.

"Diana (Mythology)." Wikipedia: The Free Encyclopedia. Wikimedia Foundation Inc. Accessed September 12, 2016. https://en.wikipedia.org/wiki/diana_(mythology).

Dietsch, D., and Robert A. M. Stern. "Greek Architecture: Doric, Ionic, Or Corinthian?" Dummies.com http://www.dummies.com/How-To/Content/Greek-Architecture-Doric-Ionic-Or-Corinthian.html.

"Discobolus." Wikipedia: The Free Encyclopedia. Wikimedia Foundation Inc. Accessed September 21, 2016. https://en.wikipedia.org/wiki/discobolus.

Dusek, B. "Golden Ratio: The Secret to Aesthetics?" Creative Sagest. Accessed September 12, 2016. http://creativesagest.blogspot.com.

"Egyptian and Atlantian Origins: One Vibration." Accessed May 8, 2014 http://one-vibration.com/Group/Egyptianandatlantianorigins?commentId=2127676%3A.

"Esther Honig: Make Me Beautiful." Christina Tanios Wellness Coaching. Accessed September 12, 2016. http://christianatanios.com/ester-honig-make-me beautiful.

"Eugenics." Wikipedia: The Free Encyclopedia. Wikimedia Foundation Inc. Accessed October 1, 2016. https://en.wikipedia.org/wiki/eugenics.

Everybody Hates Angel. 2017. "How the Caucasian Race Was Created." YouTube. Accessed January 26, 2019.

Fagles, R. 1990. *The Iliad*. New York: Penguin Books.

Fagles, R. 1996. *The Odyssey*. New York: Penguin Books.

"Fibonacci Number." Wikipedia: The Free Encyclopedia. Wikimedia Foundation Inc. Accessed October 1, 2016. https://en.wikipedia.org/wiki/fibonnaci_number.

Finnan, V. n.d. "The Sistine Ceiling Michelangelo's Masterpiece." Italian Renaissance Art. Accessed October 1, 2016. http://www.italian-renaissance-art.com/sistine-ceiling.html.

Finnan, V. n.d. "Venus and Mars." Italian Renaissance Art. Accessed October 1, 2016. http://www.italian-renaissance-art.com/venus-and-mars.html.

Flying With Eagles I Learnt To Soar. "Credo Mutwa Painting/Figurines." WordPress. Accessed June 24, 2017. https://lindasmithinspiration.wordpress.com/strange-facts-of-africa/credo-mutwa-painting.

"Francois Boucher: The Toilette of Venus." Accessed June 21, 2016 http://www.bc.edu/bc_org/avp/cas/his/coreart/art/anc_bou_toil.html.

"Francis Galton." Wikipedia: The Free Encyclopedia. Wikimedia Foundation Inc. Accessed October 1, 2016. https://en.wikipedia.org/wiki/francis_galton.

"Ganguro." Wikipedia: The Free Encyclopedia. Wikimedia Foundation Inc. Accessed September 12, 2016. https://en.wikipedia.org/wiki/ganguro.

G, Christine. 2014. "8 Ideals of Beauty from Around the World." Tripbaseblog. Trip Technologies Inc. Accessed September 12, 2016. http://www.tripbase.com/blog/8-ideals-of-beauty-from-around-the-world.

"Genesis Revisited: The Adam a Slave to The Gods." Accessed August 1, 2017. http://www.theforbiddenknowledge.com/genesis/.

"Germanic Peoples." Wikipedia: The Free Encyclopedia. Wikimedia Foundation Inc. Accessed September 12, 2016. http://en.wikipedia.org/wiki/Germanic_Peoples.

"Giacomo Barozzi Da Vignola." Wikipedia: The Free Encyclopedia. Wikimedia Foundation Inc. Accessed September 21, 2016. https://en.wikipedia.org/wiki/giacomoa_barozzi_da.

"Ginevra de' Benci" Wikipedia: The Free Encyclopedia. Wikimedia Foundation Inc. Accessed September 21, 2016. https://en.wikipedia.org/wiki/ginevra de benci.

"Ginevra de' Benci." National Gallery of Art. http://www.nga.gov/content/ngaweb/collection/highlights/highlight50724.html.

Ginzberg, L. "The Fall of the Angels: The Descendants of Cain." The Fall of the Angels. http://www.sherryshriner.com/angels/legend_fallen_angels.htm.

Ginzberg, L. "Legends of the Jews: The Descendants of Cain." http://www.sherryshriner.com/angels/punishment_of_angels.htm.

Ginzberg, L. "The Punishment of The Fallen Angels." 1479. http://www.sherryshriner.com/angels/punishment_of_angels.htm

Giv65. 2013. "Why Did You Make My Skin So Dark." CNN I-Report. CNN. Accessed September 12, 2016. http://ireport.cnn.com/docs/DOC-1006296.

"Goddess." Wikipedia: The Free Encyclopedia. Wikimedia Foundation Inc. Accessed September 21, 2016. https://en.wikipedia.org/wiki/Goddess.

"Golden Ratio." Wikipedia: The Free Encyclopedia. Wikimedia Foundation Inc. Accessed September 21, 2016. https://en.wikipedia.org/wiki/golden_ratio.

"Golden Triangle." Wikipedia: The Free Encyclopedia. Wikimedia Foundation Inc. Accessed September 21, 2016. https://en.wikipedia.org/wiki/golden_triangle.

"Gomer Son of Japheth." Amazing Bible Timeline. Accessed September 12, 2016. http://amazingbibletimeline.com/blog/gomer/.

"Gomer the Gentile." Hebrew Nations: A Britam Website. Accessed September 12, 2016. http://hebrewnations.com/articles/16/gentile.html.

"Gomer." Wikipedia: The Free Encyclopedia. Wikimedia Foundation Inc. Accessed September 12, 2016. https://en.wikipedia.org/wiki/Gomer.

Gottlieb, A. 1999. *Socrates*. New York: Routledge.

Grout, James. "Aphrodite of Cnidus." "The Hippodrome at Constantinople." Encyclopedia Romana. Accessed October 2, 2016. http://penelope.uchicago.edu/~grout/encyclopaedia_romana/circusmaximus/hippodrome.html.

Grout, James. "Discobolus." "The Hippodrome at Constantinople." Encyclopaedia Romana. Accessed October 2, 2016. http://www.penelope.uchicago.edu/~grout/encyclopadia_romana/circusmaximus/hippodro.me.html.

"Grande Odalisque." Wikipedia: The Free Encyclopedia. Wikimedia Foundation Inc. Accessed September 21, 2016. https://en.wikipedia.org/wiki/grande_odalisque.

"The Grande Odalisque." Web Gallery of Art. Accessed September 12, 2016. http://wga.hu/frames-e.html?/html/i/05ingres.html.

Guisepsi, R. A. "The Renaissance: Beginning and Progress of the Renaissance." History World International. http://history-world.org/renaissance.htm.

Heaney, M. 1994. *Over Nine Waves: A Book of Irish Legends*. London: Faber and Faber.

"Helen of Troy." Wikipedia: The Free Encyclopedia. Wikimedia Foundation Inc. Accessed September 21, 2016. https://en.wikipedia.org/wiki/Helen_Of_Troy.

Hellier, C. "Nazi Racial Ideology Was Religious, Creational and Opposed to Darwinism." Coelsblog. Http://coelsblog.wordpress.com/2011/11/08/Nazi-Racial-Ideology-Was-Religious-Creationist.

"Hippomenes." Wikipedia: The Free Encyclopedia. Wikimedia Foundation Inc. Accessed September 21, 2016. https://en.wikipedia.org/wiki/hippomenes.

"History of Minoan Crete." Ancient-Greece.org. Accessed September 12, 2016. http://ancient-greece.org/history/minoan.html.

"History of the Uyghyr People." Wikipedia: The Free Encyclopedia. Wikimedia Foundation Inc. Accessed September 12, 2016. https://en.wikipedia.org/wiki/History_Of_The_Uyghur_People.

The Holy Bible. 1976. Nashville, Tennessee: Thomas Nelson Publishers.

Hong, T., Lim Kia Mian, and Wong Rui Xiong. 2011. "History of the Science of Beauty." SlideShare. LinkedIn Corporation.Accessed September 12, 2016. http://www.Slideshare.net/Ruixiong89/Theory-Of-Beauty.

Hotep, A. 2009. "Black Skin Is the Genetic Parent." Stewart Synopsis. Last modified May 10, 2014. http://www.stewartsynopsis.com/black_skin_is_the_genetic_parent.htm.

Hotep, A. 2009. "What White People Don't Want You to Understand." Stewart Synopsis. Last modified May 10, 2014. http://www.stewartsynopsis.com/what_white_people_don.htm.

"Human Beauty." Aryanism: Unity Through Nobility. Aryanism. Accessed September 12, 2016. http://aryanism.net/culture/aesthetics/human-beauty/.

"Humanism." Wikipedia: The Free Encyclopedia. Wikimedia Foundation Inc. Accessed October 1, 2016. https://en.wikipedia.org/Humanism.

"Imperialism." Wikipedia: The Free Encyclopedia. Wikimedia Foundation Inc. Accessed September 21, 2016. https://en.wikipedia.org/wiki/imperialism.

"Iris (Mythology)." Wikipedia: The Free Encyclopedia. Wikimedia Foundation Inc. Accessed September 21, 2016. https://en.wikipedia.org/wiki/iris_(mythology).

Isvasco. "20 Most Handsome Men in Classic Hollywood." IMDb. Accessed September 12, 2016. http://www.imdb.com/list/ls006449039/.

Icke, D. "The Reptilian Blood Legacy." Reptilian Agenda. http://www.bibliotecapleyades.net/Sumer_Anunnaki/Reptiles/Reptiles30.htm.

Jefferson, Y. "Facial Beauty/Divine Proportion." Facial Beauty. Digital Xpressions. Accessed September 12, 2016. http://www.facialbeauty.org/divineproportion.html

Jesus4TrueFreedom. 2008. "MalcomX: Who Taught You to Hate Yourself?" YouTube. Accessed September 12, 2016.

Jones, J. 2016. "The Secret of Mona Lisa's Smile Lies in Leonardo's Painting." The Guardian News and Media Limited. Accessed October 1, 2016. https://www.theguardian.com/artanddesign/johnathanjonesblog/2012/oct/04/mona-lisa-leon.html.

"Judgement of Paris." Wikipedia: The Free Encyclopedia. Wikimedia Foundation Inc. Accessed September 21, 2016. https://en.wikipedia.org/wiki/Judgement_Of_Paris.

"Jupiter and Antiope (Watteau)." Wikipedia: The Free Encyclopedia. Wikimedia Foundation Inc. Accessed September 21, 2016. https://en.wikipedia.org/wiki/Jupiter_And_Antiope_(Watteau).

Kanter, T. 2013. "Maori Women in New Zealand." My Official Blog to All Rhetoric and Civic Life. RCL Blog. Accessed February 12, 2016. http://Sites.Psu.Edu/Kantner/2013/04/15/Pas-5-maori-Women-In-New-Zealand/.

Kavanagh, G. 2012. "The Sleeping Beauty of Loulan." Listverse. Accessed September 12, 2012. http://listverse.com/2012/11/01/The-Sleeping-Beauty-Of-Loulan/.

Keychain Films. 2012. "Mysterious Kalash: The Story Untold." YouTube. Accessed September 12, 2016.

"Kouros." Wikipedia: The Free Encyclopedia. Wikimedia Foundation Inc. Accessed September 12, 2016. https://en.wikipedia.org/wiki/Kouros.

"Kouros." The J. Paul Getty Museum. The J. Paul Getty Trust. Accessed September 12, 2016. http://www.getty.edu/art/collection/objects/10930/unknown-maker-kouros-greek-about-53.

Kren, E., and Daniel Marx. "Mars and Venus." Web Gallery of Art. Accessed October 1, 2016. http://www.wga.hu/html_m/b/botticel/5allegor/40venusm.html.

Kripke, D. 2013. "We Wilt in the Dark: Brighten Your Life." Brighten Your Life. Accessed September 12, 2016. http://brightenyourlife.info/.

"Kritios Boy." Wikipedia: The Free Encyclopedia. Wikimedia Foundation Inc. Accessed September 21, 2016. https://en.wikipedia.org/wiki/Kritios_Boy.

Kulke, U., and Die Welt. 2013. "How Did Blonde Whites Arrive in Peru Before Columbus?" American Renaissance. New Century Foundation. Accessed September 12, 2016. http://www.amren.com/news/2013/09/how-did-blonde-whites-arrive-in-peru-before-columbus/.

"Laocoon and His Sons." Art Encyclopedia. http://www.visual-arts-cork.com/sculpture/laocoon.htm.

"Laocoön and His Sons." Wikipedia: The Free Encyclopedia. Wikimedia Foundation Inc. Accessed September 21, 2016. https://en.wikipedia.org/wiki/Laoco%C3%B6n_and_His_Sons.

Ligon, C. 2012. "This Beautiful World: Standards of Beauty Around the World." Her Campus Media LLC. http://www.Hercampus.com/school/Tulane/Beautiful-World-Standards-Beauty-Around-World.

"Lisa del Giocondo." Wikipedia: The Free Encyclopedia. Wikimedia Foundation Inc. October 1, 2016. https://en.wikipedia.org/wiki/Lisa_Del_Giocondo.

Livingstone, D. 2002. *The Dying God: The Hidden History of Western Civilization*. http://www.thedyinggod.com/aryan-myth.

Lubin, R. 2016. "Beauty Company in Race Row over Advert That Says: 'Just Being White, You Will Win.'" Mirror. Accessed September 12, 2016. http://www.mirror.co.uk/news/world-news/beauty-company-race-row-over-7139044.

"Lucifer." Wikipedia: The Free Encyclopedia. Wikimedia Foundation Inc. Accessed October 1, 2016. https://en.wikipedia.org/wiki/Lucifer.

"The Maasai: The Authentic People of Kenya." The Maasai Tribe. Kenya Information Guide. Accessed September 12, 2016. http://www.kenya-information-guide.com/maasai-tribe.html.

Malhotra, R. 2011. "European Misappropriation of Sanskrit Led to the Aryan Race Theory." HuffPost. The Huffington Post Inc. Accessed September 12, 2016. http://www.huffingtonpost.com/rajiv-malhotra/how-europeans-misappropriation_b_837376.html.

Mandelbaum, A. 1993. *The Metamorphoses of Ovid.* New York: Harvest Book.

"Many of Their Hybrid Creations Had Blonde Hair and Blue Eyes." Above Top Secrets. The Above Network LLC. http://www.abovetopsecrets.com/forum/thread28003/pg1.

"Marlene Dietrich." Wikipedia: The Free Encyclopedia. Wikimedia Foundation Inc. Accessed September 12, 2016. https://en.wikipedia.org/wiki/Marlene_Dietrich.

"Mars and Venus." Wikipedia: The Free Encyclopedia. Wikimedia Foundation Inc. Accessed October 1, 2016. https://en.wikipedia.org/wiki/Lisa_Del_Giocondo.

"Master Race." Wikipedia: The Free Encyclopedia. Wikimedia Foundation Inc. Accessed September 21, 2016. https://en.wikipedia.org/wiki/Master_Race.

"Mathematical Beauty" The Free Encyclopedia. Wikimedia Foundation, Inc. 28 June 2016. Web. 21 Sept 2016. https://en.wikipedia.org/Wiki/Mathematical_Beauty.

"Maya Sun." Living Maya Time–Smithsonian Institution. Accessed October 1, 2016. http://maya.nmai.si.edu/maya-sun.

McCutcheon, M. 1998. *Roget's Super Thesaurus* (second ed.). Cincinnati, Ohio: Writer's Digest Books.

"Meet the Black Brazilian Mother Who Has Three White Children." Mail Online. Associated Newspapers Ltd. Accessed September 12, 2016. http://www.dailymail.co.uk/news/article-1210632/Meet-black-Brazilian-Mother-albino-children.html.

Mercatante, A. 1988. *The Facts on File Encyclopedia of World Mythology and Legend* (first ed.). New York: Facts on File.

"Metamorphoses." Wikipedia: The Free Encyclopedia. Wikimedia Foundation Inc. Accessed September 21, 2016. https://en.wikipedia.org/wiki/Metamorphoses.

"Metamorphoses." SparkNotes. SparkNotes LLC. Accessed September 12, 2016. http://www.sparknotes.com/lit/metamorphoses/Summary.html.

Merten, S. "Fallen Angel: Morning Star, Nebuchadnezzar, King of Babylon." http://www.apocalypseangel.com/morningstar.html

"Michelangelo." Wikipedia: The Free Encyclopedia. Wikimedia Foundation Inc. Accessed September 21, 2016. https://en.wikiquote.org/wiki/Michelangelo.

"Michelangelo Quotes." Brainy Quote. Accessed September 12, 2016 http://brainyquote.com/Quotes/Authors/M/Michelangelo.html.

"Minerva Protects Pax from Mars." The National Gallery. Accessed September 12, 2016. http://www.nationalgallery.org.uk/paintings/peter-paul-rubens-minevra-protects-pax-from-mars-peace-and-war.

"Minoan Art." Ancient-Greece.org. Accessed September 12, 2016. http://Ancient-Greece.org/art/minoan-art.html.

"Minoan Culture." Ancient-Greece.org. Accessed September 12, 2016. http://ancient-greece.org/culture/minoan-cult.html.

"Miss America." Wikipedia: The Free Encyclopedia. Wikimedia Foundation Inc. Accessed September 12, 2016. https://en.wikipedia.org/wiki/Miss_America.

Mittechtv. 2011. "Optogenetics: Controlling the Brain with Light." YouTube. Accessed September 12, 2016.

"Mona Lisa." Encyclopedia Britannica. Encyclopedia Britannica Inc 2016. Accessed October 1, 2016. http://www.britannica.com/topic/mona-lisa-painting.

Morgan, M. 1914. *Vitruvius: The Ten Books on Architecture*. New York: Dover Publications Inc.

"Morpheus (Mythology)." Wikipedia: The Free Encyclopedia. Wikimedia Foundation Inc. Accessed September 21, 2016. https://en.wikipedia.org/wiki/Morpheus_(Mythology).

"Morpheus and Iris." Web Gallery of Art. Accessed September 12, 2016. http://www.wga.hu/html_m/g/guerin/24morphe.html

"Myron." Wikipedia: The Free Encyclopedia. Wikimedia Foundation Inc. Accessed September 21, 2016. https://en.wikipedia.org/wiki/Myron.

Nardo, D. 2012. *The Green Haven Encyclopedia of Greek and Roman Mythology*. San Diego, California: Greenhaven Press Inc.

"Nazi Racial Ideas and Anti-Semitism." The Holocaust Explained. The Wiener Library. Accessed September 12, 2016. http://www.theholocaustexpalined.org/ks3/anti-semitism/nazi-racial-ideas-and-antisemitism.

"Nazi Racism." The Holocaust: A Learning Site for Students. United Stated Holocaust Memorial Museum, Washington DC. Accessed September 12, 2016. http://www.ushmm.org/out-reach/en/article.php?moduled=100007679.

"Neanderthal." Wikipedia: The Free Encyclopedia. Wikimedia Foundation Inc. Accessed January 26, 2019. https://en.wikipedia.org/wiki/neanderthal.

"Neurotransmitters: The Real Reason We Fall in Love." HubPages. Accessed September 12, 2016. http://hubpages.com/relationships/neurolove.

"Is The Nordic Alien Species Satan's Counterfeit for the Angels?" John the Witness. Last modified July 20, 2012. http://johnthewitness.wordpress.com/2012/07/20/is-the-nordic-alien-species-satans-counterfeit-for-the-angels?.

"Norse Mythology." Wikipedia: The Free Encyclopedia. Wikimedia Foundation Inc. Accessed September 12, 2016. https://en.wikipedia.org/wiki/Norse_Mythology.

"Nymphs and Satyr." The Clark. The Clark Art Institute. http://www.clarkart.edu/Art-Pieces/6158.

"Nymphs and Satyr." Wikipedia: The Free Encyclopedia. Wikimedia Foundation Inc. Accessed September 21, 2016. https://en.wikipedia.org/wiki/Nymphs_And_Satyr.

"O'Connor, J. J., and E. F. Robertson. "Thales of Miletus." School of Mathematics and Statistics University of St. Andrews, Scotland. Accessed September 28, 2016. http://www.history.mcs.st-and.ac.uk/biographies/thales.html.

"Oedipus and the Sphinx." Wikipedia: The Free Encyclopedia. Wikimedia Foundation Inc. Accessed September 21, 2016. https://en.wikipedia.org/wiki/Oedipus_And_The_Sphinx.

"Oedipus Explaining the Enigma of the Sphinx." Louvre. Louvre Museum, Paris. http://www.louvre.fr/en/oeuvre-notices/oedipus-explaining-enigma-sphinx.

Oldenburg, A. 2013. "Julie Chen Had Plastic Surgery to Make Eyes Bigger." USA Today. USA Today Life. Accessed September 12, 2016. http://usatoday.com/story/life/people/2013/09/12/julie-chen-plastic-eye-surgery-less-chinese/2803049

"The Original Man: The Black Man." Tripod. http://jehovahhh.tripod.com/blackman2.html.

Parveen, N. "Golden Ratio and the Ancient Egypt." The Golden Ratio. The University of Georgia, Department of Mathematics and Science Education.

"Peace and War." Artble. http://www.artble.com/Artists/Peter_Paul_Rubens/Paintings/Peace_And_War.

Pegg, D. "25 Most Beautiful Skylines in the World." List 25. List 25 LLC. Accessed September 12, 2016. http://list25.com/the-25-most-beautiful-skylines-in-the-world/

"Phi in the Human Body." Sacred Geometry. http://www.Sacred-Geometry.Es/?Q=en/Content/Phi-Human-body.

"Pin-Up Model." Wikipedia: The Free Encyclopedia. Wikimedia Foundation Inc. Accessed September 12, 2016. https://en.wikipedia.org/wiki/Pin-up_Model.

"Please Explain the Lucifer Uprising. Where, When and How Did Sin Originate?" Answers2Prayer. http://www.answers2prayer.org/bible_questions/answers/satan/origin.html.

"Pleiadians/Extraterrestrial." Arcturi.com. http://Arcturi.com/PleiadianAliens.html.

"Polykleitos." Wikipedia: The Free Encyclopedia. Wikimedia Foundation Inc. Accessed September 21, 2016. https://en.wikipedia.org/wiki/Polykleitos.

"Polyxena." Wikipedia: The Free Encyclopedia. Wikimedia Foundation Inc. Accessed September 21, 2016. https://en.wikipedia.org/wiki/Polyxena.

"Polyxena." Greek Myth Index. Myth Index. Accessed September 12, 2016. http://www.mythindex.com/greek-mythology/p/polyxena.html.

Prescott, G. 2017. "Bloodlines: Let Us Make Man in Our Own Image—Who Is Us and Our?" In5D Esoteric, Metaphysical and Spiritual Database. Accessed August 1, 2017. Http://in5d.com/bloodlines-let-us-make-man-in-our-image-who-is-us-and-our/.

"Primavera." Artble. http://www.artble.com/Artists/Sandro_Botticelli/Paintings/Primavera.

Profrum. "Darth Vader: The Power of the Dark Side." YouTube. Accessed September 12, 2016.

"Pythagoras." Wikipedia: The Free Encyclopedia. Wikimedia Foundation Inc. Accessed September 21, 2016. https://en.wikiquote.org/wiki/Pythagoras.

"Raffaello Sanzio Da Urbino or Raphael Quotes." Art Quotes. Accessed September 12, 2016 http://www.art-quotes.com/auth_search.php?authid=6964#.v0c2fvkrkuk.

"The Rape of Persephone." Angelfire. Accessed September 12, 2016. http://www.angelfire.com/persephone/rapeseph.html.

"The Rape of Proserpina." Wikipedia: The Free Encyclopedia. Wikimedia Foundation Inc. Accessed September 21, 2016. https://en.wikipedia.org/wiki/The Rape_Of_Proserpina.

Rajesh, M. 2013. "India's Unfair Obsession with Lighter Skin." *The Guardian*. Guardian News and Media Limited. Accessed September 12, 2016. http://www.theguardian.com/world/shortcuts/2013/aug/14/indias-dark-obsession-fair-skin.

Rayment, W. J. 2016. "The Age of Imperialism." Accessed September 12, 2016. http://www.indepthinfo.com/History/Imperialism.html.

Redirecting. 2018. "Scientific and Biblical Evidence of Where White Skin Comes From." YouTube. Accessed January 26, 2019.

"The Renaissance." Wikipedia: The Free Encyclopedia. Wikimedia Foundation Inc. Accessed September 19, 2016. https://en.wikipedia.org/wiki/Renaissance.

The Resolution Project. 2010. "Tom Burrells Resolution Project." YouTube. Accessed September 12, 2016.

Rhodes, R. 2013. "How Did Lucifer Fall and Become Satan." http://www.christianity.com/wiki/angels-and-demons/how-did-lucifer-fall-and-become-satan-11557519.html.

"Robert Boyle." Wikipedia: The Free Encyclopedia. Wikimedia Foundation Inc. Accessed September 21, 2016. https://en.wikipedia.org/wiki/Robert_Boyle.

Rudolph of Germany. 2015. "White People Are Not Human: Part 1". YouTube. Accessed September 12, 2016.

Rogers, L. 2008. "A Brief History of Time Measurement." University of Cambridge. http://nrich.maths.org/6070.

Rosenberg, D. 1999. *World Mythology: An Anthology of the Greatest Myths and Epics* (third edition). Lincolnwood, Illinois: NTC Publishing Group.

Rye, A. "Part 1: Ashes of Angels." The Book of Enoch and UFOs. Http://www.bibliotecapleyades.net/Enoch/Esp_enoch_7.html.

Reinckens, R. "Satan. The Devil and Demons—the Fallen Angels." God on the Net.

Sanghi, A. 2008. "Cultural Loot." 2nd Look: Aryan Achievements. WordPress. Accessed September 12, 2016. https://2ndlook.Wordpress.com/Tag/Aryan-Achievements/.

"Satan Is King of Tyre." Heaven Awaits. WordPress. http://heaven-awaits.wordpress.com/Satan-Is-King-Of-Tyre/.

Savatore Crooks. 2017. "Ancient Americans Peruvian Chachapoyas Cloud People Cultural Diffusion Long before Columbus." YouTube. Accessed September 12, 2016.

"The Science of Love." Bristol. Bristol Science Centre. Accessed September 12, 2016. http://www.youramazingbrain.org/lovesex/sciencelove.html.

"Scientific Racism." Wikipedia: The Free Encyclopedia. Wikimedia Foundation Inc. Accessed September 21, 2016. https://en.wikipedia.org/wiki/Scientific_Racism.

"Seasonal Affective Disorder." Wikipedia: The Free Encyclopedia. Wikimedia Foundation Inc. Accessed September 19, 2016. https://en.wikipedia.org/wiki/Seasonal_Affective_Disorder.

"Separation of Light from Darkness." Wikipedia: The Free Encyclopedia. Wikimedia Foundation Inc. Accessed October 1, 2016. https://en.wikipedia.org/wiki/Separation_Of_Light_From_Darkness.

"Serotonin." Wikipedia: The Free Encyclopedia. Wikimedia Foundation Inc. Accessed September 19, 2016. https://en.wikipedia.org/wiki/Serotonin.

Shriner, S. "In the Beginning: Pre-Adamic Civilization." http://www.hiddencodes.com/Sherry/In-The-Beginning.htm.

Shriner, S. "The Difference between Fallen Angels, Demons, Aliens, Jedi, and the Watchers." http://www.thewatcherfiles.com/Sherry/Who-Is-What.html.

Shriner, S. "The Serpent and the Illuminati." The Watcherflies. http://www.sherryshriner.com/sherry/serpent-illuminati.html.

"The Sistine Madonna." Art Encyclopedia. http://www.visual-arts-cork.com/famous-paintings/sistine-madonna.html.

"Sistine Madonna." Wikipedia: The Free Encyclopedia. Wikimedia Foundation Inc. Accessed October 1, 2016. https://en.wikipedia.org/wiki/Sistine_Madonna.

Sitchin, Z. 1990. "The Adam: A Slave Made to Order." Genesis Revisited. Accessed August 1, 2017. http://www.bibliotecapleyades.net/sitchin/genesisrevisto/genrevisit08.htm.

Soberana, E. 2013. "The Face of Classical Europe: Were the Greeks Blonde and Blue Eyed." Chechar WordPress. Accessed September 12, 2016. http://cienciologia.wordpress.com/category/were-the-greeks-blonde-and-blue-eyed/.

"Solar Deity." Wikipedia: The Free Encyclopedia. Wikimedia Foundation Inc. Accessed September 19, 2016. https://en.wikipedia.org/wiki/Solar_Deity.

"Sons of Elohim." Yahweh's Restoration Ministry. Accessed September 12, 2016. http://yrm.org/sons_Of_Elohim.htm.

Sribhibhadh, N. 2008. "A Westernized Standard of Beauty?" University of Washington. Accessed July 7, 2016. http://www.com.washington.edu/commir/vol2/editionthree/featuresribhibhadh.html.

"Stephen R. Marquardt." Wikipedia: The Free Encyclopedia. Wikimedia Foundation Inc. Accessed September 21, 2016. https://en.wikipedia.org/wiki/Stephen_R_Marquardt.

Strathern, P. 1997. *Socrates in 90 Minutes*. Chicago: Ivan R. Dee Inc.

Sutherland, Mary. "The History of the Red Haired Race: Tuatha de Danaan." Burlington News Website. Accessed September 12, 2016. http://www.bibliotecapleyades.net/ciencia/ciencia_tuathadedanaan04.htm.

Szalay, J. 2017. "Neanderthals: Facts About Our Extinct Human Relatives." Live Science. Accessed January 26, 2019. http://www.livescience.com/28036-neanderthals-facts-about-our-extinct-human-relatives.html.

"The Table of Nations." The Table of Nations. Sound Christian. Accessed September 12, 2016. http://www.bibliotecapleyades.net/sitchinbooks03_03a.htm.

Talent Mass Media. 2015. "Spirit of Asia: Who Are the Uyghur?" YouTube. Accessed September 12, 2016.

Tartan, S. 2013. "Uyghur People: DNA." YouTube. Accessed September 12, 2016.

TEDx Talks. 2015. "Lighting Up the Brain: Adam Cohen—TedxCambridge." YouTube. Accessed September 12, 2016.

"Theory: The Anunnaki: Enki and Enlil." The Rh-Negative Registry. Accessed August 1, 2017. http://www.rhnegativeregistry.com/the-annunaki-enki-and-enlil-rh-negative-origin.html.

"Thales." Wikipedia: The Free Encyclopedia. Wikimedia Foundation Inc. Accessed Oct 1, 2016. https://en.wikipedia.org/wiki/Thales.

"The Three Graces." Totally History. Accessed September 12, 2016. http://TotallyHistory.com/The-Three-Graces/.

"The Three Graces." Web Gallery of Art. http://www.wga.hu/Frames-e.html?html/R/Raphael/2firenze/1/21graces.html.

Tim. 2012. "Darwin's Nazi Racist Textbook: The Origin of the Species." Eternal Vigilance. Accessed September 12, 2016. http://blog.Eternalvigilance.me/2012/07/Darwins-Nazi-Textbook-The-Origin-Of-The-species/.

"Titian and the Late Renaissance in Venice." National Gallery of Art, Washington DC. http://www.nga.gov/collection/gallery/gg23-1223.html.

"The Toilette of Venus." The Met. The Metropolitan Museum. Accessed September 12, 2016. http://www.metmuseum.org/Art/Collection/Search/435739.

"The Toilet of Venus." Web Gallery of Art. Accessed September 12, 2016. http://www.wga.hu/html_m/b/boucher/2/venus_to.htm.

"Toupee Tossing." Tokyo Times. http://wordpress.tokyotimes.org/Toupee-Tossing.

"Transcript of Untitled Prezi Greece: Classical/Canonic Orders." Prezi. Prezi Inc. Accessed September 12, 2016. http://Prezi.com/Du1zihxqmnur/Untitled-prezi/.

Trask, S. 2003. "Blondes through the Ages." American Renaissance. New Century Foundation. Accessed September 12, 2016. http://www.amren.com/News/2008/12/Blondes_Through/.

"Trojan War." Wikipedia: The Free Encyclopedia. Wikimedia Foundation Inc. Accessed September 21, 2016. https://en.wikipedia.org/wiki/Trojan_War.

"Tuatha Dé Danann." Wikipedia: The Free Encyclopedia. Wikimedia Foundation Inc. Accessed September 12, 2016. https://en.wikipedia.org/wiki/Tuatha_D%C3%A9_Danaan.

"Tuscan Order." Wikipedia: The Free Encyclopedia. Wikimedia Foundation Inc. Accessed September 21, 2016. https://en.wikipedia.org/wiki/Tuscan_Order.

"*Twenty-Five Countries Photoshop Ester Honig to Make Her Beautiful.*" *Designboom*. Accessed September 12, 2016. http://www.designboom.com/art/25-countries-photoshop-esther-honig-make-her-beautiful-06-26-2014.

"Uyghurs." Wikipedia: The Free Encyclopedia. Wikimedia Foundation Inc. Accessed September 12, 2016. https://en.wikipedia.org/wiki/History_Of_The_Uyghur_People.

Vat 19. 2007. "Mona Lisa—Why So famous." YouTube. Accessed October 1, 2016.

"Venus and Adonis (Titan, Madrid)." Wikipedia: The Free Encyclopedia. Wikimedia Foundation Inc. Accessed September 21, 2016. https://en.wikipedia.org/wiki/Venus_And_Adonis_(Titan,Madrid).

"Venus Victrix (Canova)." Wikipedia: The Free Encyclopedia. Wikimedia Foundation Inc. Accessed September 21, 2016. https://en.wikipedia.org/wiki/Venus_Victrix_(Canova).

"Virtue & Beauty: Leonardo's Ginevra de' Benci and Renaissance Portraits of Women." National Gallery of Art. http://www.nga.gov/exhibitions/2001/virtuebeauty/vbintro.shtm.

"Vitruvius." Wikipedia: The Free Encyclopedia. Wikimedia Foundation Inc. Accessed September 21, 2016. https://en.wikipedia.org/wiki/Vitruvius.

"Vitruvius's Theories of Beauty." The British Library Board. Accessed September 12, 2016. http://www.bl.uk/learning/cult/bodies/vitruvius/proportion.html.

Watson, J. 2016. "Beauty Adorns Virtue." CreationSwap. CreationSwap LLC. Accessed September 12, 2016. http://www.creationswap.com/article/7002.

Wayne. "Understanding the Enemy: The Difference between Fallen Angels and Demons." Prophecy Proof Insights. http://prophecyproof.blogspot.com/2010/10/knowing-enemy-difference-between-fallen.html.

Weigel, J. 1991. *Mythology*. Lincoln, Nebraska: Cliff Notes.

Weiss, R. "The First Appearance of White Skin in Humans." Stewart Synopsis. Last modified February 26, 2014. http://www.stewartsynopsis.com/first_appearance_of_white_skin_i.htm.

"Westernization." Wikipedia: The Free Encyclopedia. Wikimedia Foundation Inc. Accessed September 21, 2016. https://en.wikipedia.org/wiki/Westernization.

"What Is Beauty: Definition of Beauty." Awesome Inc. Accessed September 12, 2016. http://catwalkgrl.blogspot.com/2012/02/definition-of-beauty.htm.

"What Does It Mean to Be Human?" Smithsonian National Museum of Natural History. Accessed January 26, 2019. http://humanorigins.si.edu/.

"The White Race Is Completely Alien to This Planet Because They Are Descendants from Aliens." Godlike Productions. Last modified May 8, 2014 http://www.godlikeproductions.com/forum1/Message1775981/Pg7.

"Why the Aryans Were Worshipped as Sun Gods." Godlike Productions. http://www.godlikeproductions.com/forum1/Message974175/pg1.

Wister, W. 2013. "Why Does Sunshine Make People Happy?" Quora. Accessed September 12, 2016. http://www.quora.com/Why-Does-Sunshine-Make-People-Happy.

"1–999 AD World History." Pearson Education. Infoplease. http://www.infoplease.com/ipa/A0001209.html.

Worthington, J. 2019. "20 Physical Traits You May Have Inherited from a Neanderthal." Abroad in the Yard. Accessed January 26, 2019. http://www.abroadintheyard.com/20-physical-traits-inherited-from-neanderthal/.

Yahya, H. 1994. "Darwin, Too, Was a Racist." Anti-Darwinism.com. Global Publication Ltd and Harun Yahya. Accessed September 12, 2016 http://antidarwinism.com/socialdarwinism_favordraces.html.

"Zeus." Wikipedia: The Free Encyclopedia. Wikimedia Foundation Inc. Accessed September 19, 2016. https://en.wikipedia.org/wiki/Zeus.

Zia-Ebrahim, R. 2010. "Iranian Identity: The Aryan Race and Jake Gyllenhaul." Tehran Bureau. Accessed September 12, 2016 http://www.pbs.org/wgbh/pages/frontline/tehranbureau/2010/08/post-2.html.

ABOUT THE AUTHOR

From an early age, Silas was always blessed with a gift for creativity, whether he was drawing pictures, creating modeled face figures in art class, or constructing model transportation vehicles out of cardboard. After high school, he shifted his focus to writing. As a person, Silas is thoughtful, loving, and kind, a family-oriented individual who lives in the tristate area between Delaware, Philadelphia, and New Jersey. He often travels within these areas to visit friends and family members.

www.ingramcontent.com/pod-product-compliance
Lightning Source LLC
LaVergne TN
LVHW021129160826
845679LV00015B/1688
9798891127449